Ninth Edition

A Guide to
The Cathedral Church of St. John the Divine
in the City of New York.

UNIV. OF MICH.

THE NORTH ELEVATION OF THE CATHEDRAL
(From Architect's Design)

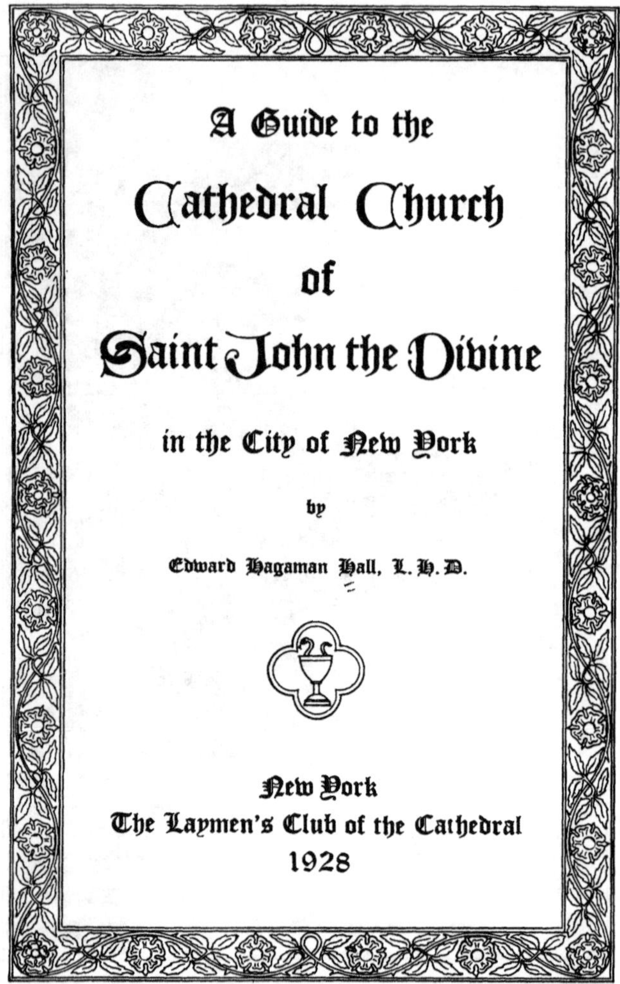

# A Guide to the Cathedral Church of Saint John the Divine in the City of New York

by

Edward Hagaman Hall, L. H. D.

New York
The Laymen's Club of the Cathedral
1928

Ninth Edition

Copyright, 1928, by
The Laymen's Club of
The Cathedral Church of St. John the Divine,
New York, N. Y.

---

Dates of publication: First edition, February, 1920; Second, June, 1920; Third, July, 1921; Fourth, December, 1922; Fifth, July, 1924; Sixth, March, 1925; Seventh, November, 1925; Eighth, October, 1926; Ninth, November, 1928. Total number of copies printed, 42,000.

# Introductory Note

This Guide to the Cathedral of Saint John the Divine purposely departs from the conventional guide book in several respects. The Cathedral of St. John the Divine is not centuries old like those in Europe, but is in the building; and it has seemed appropriate in the first place to express something of its Spirit before describing the details of its Fabric. In the next place, the great majority of visitors to the Cathedral are strangers, people of many communions, and, on account of its proximity to one of the leading American universities, students. For this reason, an effort has been made to avoid technical terms as far as possible; to explain the significance of much symbolism not generally understood; and to insert Bible references freely for the benefit of those who wish to study further the meaning of the scenes and objects described. Lest some of the explanations—as, for instance, that in regard to the probable date of the completion of the Cathedral—be deemed superfluous, it may be said that this, as well as nearly every other statement in the following pages, is an answer to some question asked among the thousand and one interrogations which manifest popular interest in the Cathedral's growth.

For their valuable co-operation in the preparation of the Guide, grateful acknowledgment is made to the Bishop, to the Dean, and to Canons George F. Nelson and Robert Ellis Jones. Many thanks for courtesies in photographing and studying the Cathedral are also due to Mr. Thomas Meatyard, the Verger.

Niche in St. Ansgarius Chapel made of old Cathedral Stones

(See page 103)

# Contents

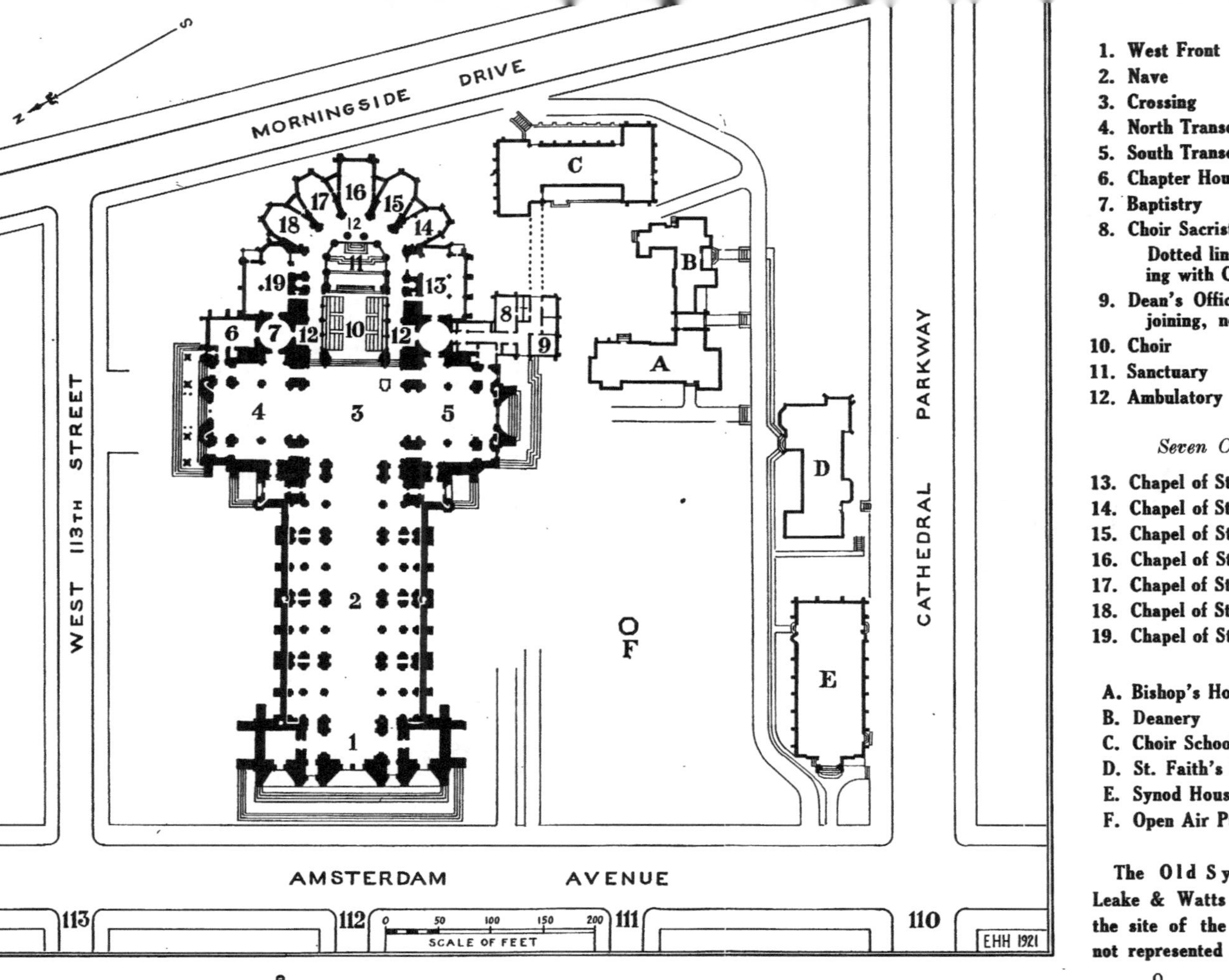




1. West Front
2. Nave
3. Crossing
4. North Transept, begun
5. South Transept, not begun
6. Chapter House, not begun
7. Baptistry
8. Choir Sacristy, not begun
   Dotted lines indicate cloisters connecting with Choir School
9. Dean's Office, with Canons' Offices adjoining, not begun
10. Choir
11. Sanctuary
12. Ambulatory

*Seven Chapels of Tongues*

13. Chapel of St. James
14. Chapel of St. Ambrose
15. Chapel of St. Martin of Tours
16. Chapel of St. Saviour
17. Chapel of St. Columba
18. Chapel of St. Boniface
19. Chapel of St. Ansgarius

---

A. Bishop's House
B. Deanery
C. Choir School
D. St. Faith's House
E. Synod House
F. Open Air Pulpit

The Old Synod House (formerly the Leake & Watts Orphan Asylum) stands on the site of the South Transept (5) and is not represented on this plan.

# Illustrations

# Part One

# The Spirit of the Cathedral

---

## The Real Cathedral

On Morningside Heights, in the City of New York, on ground consecrated by the blood of our forefathers in the War for Independence, stands a trinity of institutions which represent with singular completeness the three-fold nature of man: Columbia University, which ministers to the Mind; St. Luke's Hospital, which ministers to the Body; and the Cathedral of St. John the Divine, which ministers to the Soul.

This little book is designed to assist visitors to understand the meaning and purpose of the Cathedral of St. John the Divine. Some such aid, either written or oral, is needed, for a great cathedral cannot be comprehended in the glance of an eye. Certain features, such as its magnitude and general beauty, are obvious; but inwrought with these is a wealth of meaning which is the *soul* of the Cathedral — the *real* Cathedral — and which reveals itself only on intimate acquaintance. When Ruskin called Amiens Cathedral "The Bible of Amiens," he used a figure of speech applicable to all cathedrals. The Cathedral of St. John the Divine is "The Word in stone." It is a sacred book, written in massive pier and ponderous arch, in sculptured marble and carved oak, in stained glass window and inlaid mosaic, in embroidered fabric and woven tapestry, whose pages are full of delight, inspiration and help for those who will take the trouble to read them.

The Cathedral performs its function as a place for the praise and worship of Almighty God in two ways—statically in the grandeur and beauty of the temple, and actively in the services held within it.

## Praise in its Greatness

Like other great cathedrals, St. John the Divine first impresses by its size. Its magnitude is not only becoming to its rank as the chief church of the great Diocese of New York and necessary for the accommodation of large congregations, but it also has a spiritual purpose, for it gives one the feeling of something bigger than one's self and of a Power greater than one's own. "The Cathedral gives me a feeling of humility," said a man to Bishop Greer one day. "When I go in," said a college girl to him, "I forget myself." And a man whom the Bishop met in the Ambulatory said to him: "If I came here regularly, something about it,—its size, its spaciousness, its loftiness, its great receding Choir—something about it would compel me to be a churchman."

## Praise in its Beauty

The Cathedral is designed also to praise God in the glory of its Beauty. Ruskin, in "The Laws of Fesole," says that "all great art is praise." Here we have the three great and enduring arts of Architecture, Sculpture and Painting (the latter including stained glass), combined in a wonderful Te Deum of Beauty. For centuries the great cathedrals of the world have been the caskets of certain kinds of art—or, rather, of certain kinds of expression of art—not elsewhere to be found; and in this respect the Cathedral of St. John the Divine fills a place in our American life which no secular building can fill. In the beauty of its general form, in the beauty of its detail, in the beauty of its symbolism, and in the record of human achievement in godly living which these express, the Cathedral stirs the most reverent emotions and creates the noblest aspirations.

## Praise in its Service

But these silent though eloquent physical features are only adjuncts and helps to the active expression of praise in the Cathedral Service. In this, the impressive rites of the church and the congregational participation are aided by music brought to a high degree of perfection, and the preaching from the pulpit aims to interpret the Christian religion in terms of the practical every-day life of to-day.

In short, the Cathedral endeavors to employ all that is beautiful and majestic in Art and Service to bring God closer to men and to draw men closer to God.

Those who live near enough to the Cathedral to be able to attend its services frequently can appreciate the words of a man who lived most of his life in one of the great cathedral towns of England, and who said:

"I account it one of the greatest blessings of my life, and a circumstance which gave a tone to my imagination which I would not resign for many earthly gifts, that I lived in a place where the cathedral service was duly and beautifully performed. . . . If the object of devotion be to make us *feel,* and to carry away the soul from all earthly thoughts, assuredly the grand chaunts of our cathedral service are not without their use. I admire—none can admire more—the abstract idea of an assembly of reasoning beings offering up to the Author of all good things their thanksgivings in a pure and intelligible form of words; but the question will always intrude, Does the heart go along with this lip service? and is the mind sufficiently excited by this reasonable worship to forget its accustomed associations with the business and vanities and passions of the world? The cathedral service *does* affect the imagination and through that channel the heart."

## The Spirit of Democracy

While the Cathedral of St. John the Divine is a Protestant Episcopal Cathedral, its ministrations are not restricted. "Our democratic age," said Bishop Henry C. Potter, "demands a place of worship that will not disregard the teachings of the Founder of Christianity. In this Cathedral there will be no pews, no locked doors, no pre-payment for sittings, no reserved rights of caste or rank, but one and the same welcome for all." And what Bishop Potter prophesied when the Cathedral was first planned is literally true to-day. The charter of the Cathedral requires that "the seats for worshippers in said Cathedral Church shall always be free;" and the Cathedral welcomes everybody to its services, irrespective of denominational affiliations, nationality or worldly estate. The Cathedral also welcomes those who belong to no denomination. Its appeal to the latter was particularly contemplated when Bishop Potter said: "The person in the period of suspense as to certain fundamental beliefs needs something larger, higher, wider and roomier, more impersonal for the time being, than the parish church." It is hardly necessary to add as a corollary of the foregoing that there are no "strangers' pews" in the Cathedral; and nobody, however unaccustomed to the Cathedral service, needs to feel any timidity or hesitation about attending. The large proportion of men in the Cathedral congregations is particularly noticeable.

## A Civic Institution

In its present state of incompletion, the capacity of the Cathedral is taxed to the utmost limits, and on special occasions thousands are turned away unable to enter. The completion of the Cathedral is therefore imperative; and this is so for more than denominational reasons, for the many notable special services held during the past few years and participated in by people of all denominations already indicate the position which it is destined to occupy as a great Civic and National Institution. The Board of Trustees recently said: "The city requires a religious edifice where people can gather together in large numbers to express in a corporate way their religious promptings and to find spiritual interpretation of great events." Such were the gatherings—to mention but a few typical instances—on several occasions following the World War, such as the Thanksgiving for peace, the Thanksgiving of the twelve Liberated Nationalities, the Lusitania memorial service, the memorial services for the dead (Gounod's "Life and Death" and Dvorak's "Requiem"); also the services in memory of Presidents Harding and Wilson, and, more recently, the extraordinary series of Evangelistic services in Lent, 1925, the remarkable Labor Sunday service in September, 1925, services at various times for the Grand Lodge of Free Masons, the Knights Templars, the Y. W. C. A., the Gold Star Mothers, the Trained Nurses, the Firemen of the City of New York, the Letter Carriers of the City, the historical and patriotic societies, etc., the Beethoven Centennial in March, 1927, and the service in memory of Field Marshal Haig on February 19, 1928. In these special services, clergymen and lay speakers of other denominations are frequently invited to take part.

People rarely think of the English cathedrals as belonging to the Church of England or of the French cathedrals as belonging to the Roman Catholic church. They are regarded as belonging to everybody. And such, it is believed, is the place which the Cathedral of St. John the Divine will occupy in the minds of the people of the city and nation.

## A Great Symbol

The symbolism of various details of the Cathedral will be mentioned hereafter; but it should be said here that the Cathedral as a whole is a great and wonderful symbol. "The religion which is inwrought with all the history of the American people," said Bishop Potter, "stands for certain lofty ideals of truth, purity, honesty, loyalty and self-sacrifice. Every ideal must have some visible expression or symbol, and this ideal of our religious faith from the very nature of it demands expression, incarnation, visible and material utterance worthy of its majesty and grandeur." And the Trustees not long ago said: "New York is the chief city of the Western World. It impresses the imagination at every turn by visible evidence of the power and splendor of material achievements in American life. Such a city should be dominated by a building which, in its greatness, dignity and beauty, bears witness to those spiritual forces without which material achievement is valueless because soulless."

## A Sign of Stability

This ever-changing city also needs the Cathedral as an evidence of stability. Business structures and apartment houses rise and disappear in a generation under the exigencies of the city's growth. Even parish churches give way under this seemingly irresistible pressure. There is consequently little upon which to fasten permanently one's memories, affections and historical traditions. Amid the changes and uncertainties of human life, man instinctively looks to the Church for something of permanence—something after all to which he can fasten his faith and upon which he can anchor his hopes. The Cathedral of St. John the Divine, resting in its massive solidity upon the ancient rocks of Morningside Heights, gives an idea of firmness and stability in contrast with the fleeting changes around it and symbolizes Eternity as nearly as anything erected by the hands of man can. It will stand for unmeasured time as an eloquent memorial of the best and noblest of human effort and will serve as a visible bond to bind together generations of high endeavor. "A cathedral," said Dean Robbins in a sermon on December 17, 1916, "is a symbol of continuity of life through the ages. It is a reminder of the relatedness in which men stand not only to one another but also to those who have preceded them, to all that is still memorable in a not quite vanished past." And looking to the future he spoke of the meaning of the Cathedral to coming generations when it should have become adorned with associations growing like ivy over walls made venerable by time. "Perhaps they will be greater memories, more glorious associations, than our best hopes can now forecast. . . . Who can tell what the hidden, wonderful, all-possible future may have in store for our Cathedral, what hopes and purposes and sorrows and rejoicings will receive their consecration within its slowly aging walls?"

THE CATHEDRAL, BISHOP'S HOUSE, DEANERY AND CHOIR SCHOOL

# Part Two

# The Fabric of the Cathedral

---

## Name and Namesake

The legal title of the Cathedral is "the Cathedral Church of Saint John the Divine in the City and Diocese of New York." The adjective "cathedral," commonly used as a noun, is derived from the Greek word "cathedra" which means "seat." In the Cathedral is the cathedra of the Bishop of the Diocese of New York. It is not a parish church and has no members in the sense in which a parish church has members; but persons desiring to assist in cathedral work may join the auxiliary organizations mentioned on page 131 following. The Cathedral is the chief church of the Diocese which embraces 294 different parishes and missions.

The Cathedral is named after the author of the fourth Gospel, the three "epistles general" bearing the name of John, and the book of "The Revelation of St. John the Divine." The word "Divine" in the title is not an adjective* but is a noun in apposition with "St. John" and is rendered in the seal of the Cathedral by the Latin word "theologus," meaning "theologian." St. John was one of the twelve Apostles, and a brother of St. James the Great. He was "the Disciple whom Jesus loved" (John xiii. 23), an expression implying exceptional sweetness and lovableness of character. He founded the

---

* The quality of divinity appertaining only to the Deity.

seven churches in Asia referred to in the Book of Revelation. Toward the end of his ministrations, in which he suffered many persecutions, he was banished to the Isle of Patmos, where he wrote the Book of Revelation. When he returned from this exile, he continued his work until he died at the advanced age of over 90 years. His traditional grave is at Ephesus. The two principal symbols of St. John are the eagle with book, (explained in connection with the symbols of the four Evangelists on page 111) and the chalice, the latter sometimes having a serpent issuing from it. The sacramental cup without the serpent is sometimes interpreted to refer to Christ's reply to James and John: "Ye shall indeed drink of the cup that I drink of" (Mark x. 39). The cup with the serpent refers to the tradition related by St. Isidore to the effect that at Rome an attempt was made to poison St. John in the communion wine, but that by a miracle the poison vanished from the chalice in the form of a serpent. The Memorial Day for St. John is kept on December 27.

## Location and Access

The Cathedral is located between Cathedral parkway (110th street), Amsterdam avenue, 113th street, and Morningside drive.

The Cathedral can be reached by taking the Broadway subway to 110th street and walking one block east and two north; the Broadway surface line to 112th street and walking one block east; the Amsterdam avenue surface line to the entrance at 112th street; the 6th and 9th avenue elevated line to 110th street and walking two blocks west and two north; or Fifth avenue omnibuses marked route "4" via 110th street, or 'buses transferring thereto.

Morningside Heights being 100 feet above the level of the adjacent Harlem Plain, the Cathedral commands a sweeping prospect toward the northeast, east, and south-east, over the roofs of the city and past the trees of Central Park to the regions beyond the Harlem and East rivers; while from the main entrance at Amsterdam avenue and 112th street, one can look westward to the Hudson and see the columned Palisades on the New Jersey shore beyond. Morningside Heights is the modern name for the ground on which the battle of Harlem Heights was fought on September 16, 1776. Washington, whose figure occupies a niche in the Choir Parapet (page 52) and adorns the entrance to the Synod House (page 130), personally directed the troops in this engagement. At that period an old colonial road ran through the Cathedral site and down the Heights of Morningside Park to the ancient King's Highway or Post Road. When the Americans evacuated New York City on September 15, 1776, those who escaped by way of Bloomingdale probably passed over this road. A British map surveyed that year by Claude Joseph Sauthier shows that a column of Hessians marched over this route going to the attack on Fort Washington November 16, 1776. During the War of 1812, the Cathedral grounds were immediately within the lines of defence erected in 1814, one of the blockhouses of which stood on the bluff on the eastern side of Morningside drive just northeast of 113th st.*

The Cathedral grounds,—called the "Close," from the practice in olden times of securing the privacy of the cathedral precincts by enclosing them with a wall and gates,—comprise 11½ acres. Upon them are situated, besides the Cathedral, the Old Synod House (brick with columned portico, formerly the Leake & Watts Orphan Asylum), the Bishop's House and Deanery, the Choir School, the New Synod House, and St. Faith's Training School for Deaconesses.

---

* This was a stone tower similar to the one so well preserved in Central Park. The remains of another are at the northern end of Morningside Park.

## Cathedral Staff

Following is the Cathedral Staff:

*Bishop*

The Right Rev. William Thomas Manning, D.D., D.C.L., LL.D.

*Dean*

The Very Rev. Howard Chandler Robbins, D.D.

*Canon Bursar*

The Rev. Robert Ellis Jones, D.D.

*Sacrist*

The Rev. Cranston Brenton, M.S.

*Precentor and Head Master of the Choir School*

The Rev. William Dudley Foulke Hughes, M.A., B.Litt.

*Staff Assistant*

The Rev. Joseph Buchanan Bernardin, B.D.

*Honorary Canons*

The Rev. George Francis Nelson, D.D.
The Rev. George Frederick Clover, M.A.
The Rev. Harold Adye Prichard, M.A.
The Rev. Pascal Harrower, M.A.

*Organist and Master of the Choristers*

Miles Farrow, M.A., Mus. Doc.

The post-office address of any of the above mentioned is "The Cathedral of St. John the Divine, New York, N. Y." The Bishop's office is in the Synod House. The offices of the Dean, Canon Bursar, etc., are in the old Synod House. (See page 9.)

## Seals of Diocese and Cathedral

The seal of the Diocese is in the form of a pointed oval, or vesica, and is as follows:

Quarterly *gules* and *argent,* over all a cross counterchanged of the same. In dexter chief the American eagle with wings displayed *or;* in sinister chief and dexter base the sails of a windmill *proper* from the arms of the City of New York. In sinister base two swords in saltire *or* from the arms of the see of London. Surmounted by and episcopal mitre *proper.* The arms surmounted on a field *purpure* and enclosed by a bordure *azure* lined (or edged) *or* bearing the legend "Seal of the Diocese of New York MDCCLXXXV" *or.*

Diocesan Seal

Cathedral Seal

The red color (gules) and the swords are historically reminiscent of the fact that prior to the Independence of the United States the church throughout the American Colonies was under the ecclesiastical jurisdiction of the Diocese of London. (See historical note on page 26.)

The seal of the Cathedral, also vesica-shaped, is as follows:

Tierce in pairle reversed. 1st, from the arms of the City of New York: *argent* four sails of a windmill in saltire, between the ends in chief and base a beaver couchant, in fess dexter and sinister a barrel of flour all *proper*. 2d, from the arms of the State of New York: *azure* in a landscape the sun in fess rising in splendor *or* behind a range of three mountains the middle one the highest, in base a ship and sloop under sail passing and about to meet on a river bordered below by a grassy shore fringed with shrubs all *proper*. 3d, *azure* seven six-pointed stars *argent* between as many candlesticks *or*. Surmounted by an episcopal mitre *proper*. Enclosed by a bordure *gules* edged *or* bearing the legend "Sigil. Eccles. Cath. S. Johann. Theol. N. Ebor." *or*.

The seven stars and candlesticks refer to the Revelation of St. John the Divine, i. 20.

## Services

The Cathedral is open for private prayer and meditation every day of the year from 7.30 a.m. to 6.00 p. m. The Holy Communion is celebrated in one of the chapels every week-day at 7.30 a. m. The principal Sunday services are at 8 a. m., 11 a. m. and 4 p. m., the latter two being with full choral service and sermon. Other services are held on week-days and Sundays as announced from time to time. As before stated, all seats are free, and residents and strangers of all denominations are cordially welcome.

The Cathedral service is the prescribed liturgy with choral rendering and congregational participation. Except during the vacation season, there are usually about 60 persons in the procession. The processional hymn is begun in the Ambulatory, through the south gate of which the procession enters the Crossing and goes to the Choir. First comes the crucifer, followed in order by the boys of the choir, the men of the choir, the Head Master of the Choir School, the Verger and the clergy in inverse order of their rank. The Bishop, if present, comes last, and is immediately preceded by the Verger and the Bishop's chaplain (or an acolyte) bearing the Bishop's pastoral staff. If the Bishop is absent, the Dean comes last, preceded by the Verger. If neither Bishop nor Dean is present, the Verger precedes all the clergy. *The Pastoral Staff* was given to Bishop Manning in 1923 by the Bishop, clergy and laity of the Diocese of London, as a symbol of the love and fellowship which bind together the two great branches of the Anglican Communion and which, it is hoped, will ever unite the English-speaking peoples, and has especial significance in view of the historic relations between the Diocese of London and the Diocese of New York. (See reference to the Diocese of London on page 26.) The staff is a beautiful work of art in silver, overlaid with gold and enamel, five feet and eleven inches long, modeled after the crozier of Bishop Fox of Exeter, later of Winchester. The original, made in 1490, and now preserved in Corpus Christi College, Oxford, is said by Jackson's "Illustrated History of English Plate" to be "the most splendid example of the goldsmith's work which has survived to our time." In the head, or whorl, of the staff, under a gothic canopy, are figures of St. George and the dragon and St. John with the chalice. Under these is an angel with book hovering over a pelican and nest of young. The sides of the whorl are also ornamented with pelicans. Below the whorl are two groups of six gothic niches, arranged hexagonally, containing figures of the Twelve Apostles, each with his appropriate symbol. Below these are two groups of four bosses. On the upper four are the arms of the See of New York, the arms of the See of London, the arms of the Bishop of London, and the initials of Bishop Manning, "W.T.M." On the lower four are the arms of George Washington, the arms of Charles Inglis (Assistant Rector and Rector of Trinity Parish, New York City, 1765-1783; first Bishop of Nova Scotia and first Colonial Bishop of the English Church,

1787-1816); the arms of Henry Compton (Bishop of London, 1675-1714*); and the initials of Samuel Provoost, "S.P.", (first Bishop of New York, 1787-1815). The recessional is in the same order as the processional. After entering the Ambulatory, the procession halts while a dismissal prayer or hymn is said or sung there, and the solemn service ends with a far-away "Amen" from the unseen choir.

## Visitors

Visitors may see the Cathedral at all times between 7.30 a. m. and 6.00 p. m. except during the hours of service. The Verger is usually in attendance. On Sundays, after the 11 a. m. and 4 p. m. services, the Ushers conduct groups of visitors through the Cathedral and explain its details.

## Architecture

The architects of the Cathedral have been: Messrs. George L. Heins and C. Grant LaFarge from July, 1891, until Mr. Heins' death in September, 1907; Mr. La Farge from September, 1907, until the completion of

* It may assist the reader to understand the allusion to the Diocese of London in the description of the Diocesan Seal on page 23 and the reference to Bishop Compton above and on page 111 to recall that when New Netherland was conquered by the English in 1664, the Established Church of England naturally became that of the Colony of New York. After the conquest, the Dutch and English congregations in New York City worshipped at different hours on Sunday in what had been the Dutch Church of St. Nicholas in the fort. This practice continued until 1693, when the Dutch congregation began to use its new church in Garden street. Soon thereafter steps were taken for the organization of a regular parish for the English and for the erection of a new church for them outside of the fort, and on May 6, 1697, William III. granted a charter to Trinity Parish, constituting "our right trusty and well-beloved the Right Reverend Father in God, Henry, Lord Bishop of London, and of our Privy Council, the first Rector thereof." Bishop Compton never became resident Rector of Trinity Parish, but on August 2, 1697, he ordained the Rev. William Vesey for that position. The present Bishop of this Diocese was the tenth Rector of Trinity Parish in succession to Bishop Compton and upon his election to the episcopate became the tenth Bishop of New York.

the Choir in April, 1911; and Messrs. Cram & Ferguson from April, 1911, to the present time. Mr. Henry Vaughan was architect of three of the seven Ambulatory Chapels, Messrs. Heins & LaFarge of two, Messrs. Cram & Ferguson of one and Messrs. Carrere & Hastings of one, as mentioned hereafter. Messrs. Cram & Ferguson were also architects of the Baptistery.

The prevailing style of the Cathedral is French Gothic. The north of France, it will be remembered, is the birthplace of Gothic architecture. There it rose and reached the flower of perfection in such monuments as Amiens, Rheims, Notre Dame (Paris), Chartres, Beauvais, and Rouen Cathedrals and many other churches, great and small. But, while certain features of the Cathedral of St. John the Divine suggest the older Gothic cathedrals of Europe, it is not, as Dr. Alfred D. F. Hamlin, Professor of Architecture at Columbia University, says, "a copying or archæological imitation of mediæval exemplars. The French Gothic, as here used, is handled with such originality and boldness of invention as to form a new and distinctly American chapter in its development."

## Plan and Size

The plan of the Cathedral is cruciform (symbolism, the cross on which Christ was crucified); and is oriented so that the priest standing at the High Altar faces the east (the rising sun symbolizing the resurrection, and the orientation also connoting the ideas of Christ "the Sun of Righteousness," "the Dayspring from on High," and the "Morning Star").* Seven chapels radiate from the Apse, or semi-circular eastern end of the Choir. The loftiest features of the elevation are the two towers of the West Front (q.v.) and the great Central Tower (q.v.)

* Morningside Heights are so named because they front eastward.

When completed, the Cathedral will extend from Morningside drive to Amsterdam avenue, more than a tenth of a mile. It will be 601 feet long and 315 feet wide across the Transepts, and, with an area of 109,082 square feet, will be the largest in any English-speaking country and the fourth largest in the world. (See table of comparative sizes on page 117.) The seating capacity of the Cathedral when finished will be about 10,000, with standing room for many thousands more when the chairs are removed.

The late Alfred D. F. Hamlin characterized the design for the Cathedral as "a stupendous and inspiring monument of our faith and a triumphant vindication equally of American religion and American art. . . . Nothing comparable to this superb design has ever been erected in America, and the cathedrals of Europe may fairly be challenged to surpass or even to equal it."

## Progress of Construction

The Founder of the Cathedral was the Right Rev. Horatio Potter, who proposed it in 1872. The charter was granted by the Legislature of the state of New York in 1873. The Right Rev. Henry Codman Potter, nephew and successor of Bishop Horatio Potter, actively forwarded the movement for raising funds in 1886. The Close was purchased from the Leake & Watts Orphan Asylum by deed dated October 31, 1891. The first service on the ground was held January 1, 1892. The corner-stone was laid on St. John's Day, December 27, 1892.* The first service was held in the Crypt January 8, 1899, and the first service in the Choir and Crossing (being the consecration service) April 19, 1911. Ground was broken for the Nave May 8, 1916, by the Right Rev.

* See description of corner-stone on page 106.

BUILDING THE WEST FRONT AND THE NAVE
(Photograph Taken September 24, 1928)

David Hummell Greer. Ground was broken for the West Front on May 6, 1925, by the Right Rev. William Thomas Manning, present Bishop of New York, on November 9, 1925, he laid the "foundation stone" of the Nave,† and on December 5, 1927, he presided at the breaking of ground for the North Transept. The parts thus far built are the Crypt, the Choir, the seven Ambulatory Chapels, the Baptistry and the Crossing; the West Front and Nave are nearing completion; and the North Transept is in course of construction.

## Funds for Building

Visitors to the Cathedral repeatedly ask when it will be finished. It is impossible to answer this question definitely. Some of the cathedrals of the Old World have been seven hundred years in building and are not yet completed. The things which endure the longest are generally of slow growth,* and the Cathedral of St. John the Divine is no exception to this rule. It is not a steel-frame structure, but is of massive masonry in the best traditions of Gothic architecture and is being built to stand for ages. Its physical construction must therefore necessarily be slow.

It is to be remembered, also, that the financial resources for the building of a modern cathedral are different from those which supplied the means for building many of the Old World churches. Westminster Abbey was built almost entirely from revenues of the Kings from Henry III. to Henry VII. St. Paul's in London was partly built by the gifts of penitents who performed their penances in money. Occasionally an ancient shrine grew into a great church in consequence of some tradi-

† See description and illustration of the foundation stone on page 40

***This is true in both the natural and the spiritual worlds. The oak grows more slowly than the pine; and the moral achievements which are worth the most and last the longest are the hardest to accomplish.**

tion or superstition which caused a continuous stream of illustrious persons to shower wealth, privileges and honors upon it. Pope Honorius prescribed collections in all Christendom for the building of Rheims Cathedral. The metropolitan church of St. Rombold's, in Malines, Belgium, was built with money paid by pilgrims who flocked thither in the 14th and 15th centuries to obtain indulgences issued by Pope Nicholas V.; and the Tour de Beurre (butter tower) of Bourges Cathedral, like the tower of the same name at Rouen, derives its name from having been erected with money paid for indulgences to eat butter in Lent. To-day, however, reliance is placed entirely upon voluntary contributions, and there have been many gifts, both large and small, from donors irrespective of denominational affiliations who have caught the civic and patriotic as well as the religious inspiration of what is to be America's greatest cathedral. In a general way, it may be said that the Cathedral will be finished as fast as funds are provided;—and no faster, for the authorities have rigidly maintained the provision of the statute, building only what can be paid for, and worshippers are therefore not kneeling on any debt.

Since January, 1925, a great popular movement, under the leadership of the Bishop and sponsored by a citizens' committee representing all classes of people, has been conducted to raise funds for the completion of the Cathedral. One of the most extraordinary meetings ever held in the City of New York was that held in connection with this undertaking in Madison Square Garden on Sunday evening, January 18, 1925, when 15,000 people of all denominations were present and over 5,000 more were unable to gain admittance. Under the inspiration of this movement, various groups of citizens, representing the Art, Educational, Historical and Patriotic, Military and Naval, Medical, Legal, Recreative and Athletic, Business, and Labor interests of the community, the interests of Women and those of Children, etc., have undertaken to raise funds for building certain large units of the Cathedral. One of the great arches of the Nave, called the Children's Arch, was built by pennies from children; and funds for the pavement of the Nave, called the Pilgrim's Pavement, are being raised by the Laymen's Club by contributions from visitors to the Cathedral. Gifts to the building fund range all the way from a few cents given by a newsboy or a day's wages by a workman, upward into the thousands given by those more fortunately blessed with riches. They come from Protestants, Catholics and Jews; from rich and poor; from men, women and children; from clerks, students, waitresses, working girls, working men, butlers, inmates of benevolent institutions, merchants, bankers, professional men,—every conceivable class of people. Every donor's name, no matter what the size of the gift, is to be enrolled in the Golden Book of the Cathedral. Literature concerning the personnel, organization and objectives of the Committee for Completing the Cathedral, together with detailed information concerning collective or separate features of the Cathedral toward which contributions may be made as memorials, will be sent upon request addressed to the Bishop or the Dean at the Cathedral, Amsterdam avenue and 112th street, New York City. Remittances may be sent to the Bishop or to the Treasurer of the Committee, Mr. Edward W. Sheldon, at the Cathedral. Contributions may also be placed in the alms basin at the Cathedral services, or in the box at the door.

## Foundation and Superstructure

The foundation of the Cathedral is of Maine granite and concrete. Although the bed-rock of Morningside Heights (Manhattan schist) lies near the surface, it is so disintegrated near the top that it was necessary to go down 72 feet in some places in order that the Cathedral might rest securely on the "living rock." The main walls of the superstructure are also of granite, faced on the outside with Mohegan golden granite quarried near Peekskill, N. Y., and on the inside of the eastern portion with a soft buff-colored limestone, or dolomite, called Frontenac stone, from Pepin county, Wis. The interior of the Nave is faced with Indiana limestone. The massive piers of the Crossing, exposed in their rugged unfinished state, exhibit the dark Maine granite. Local materials are mentioned in their appropriate places.

## Exterior Survey

Before entering the Cathedral the visitor should make a circuit of the Close (beginning on the south side and going eastward), comparing the outlines of the Cathedral with the plan and noting the location of the other buildings. This will give him a better understanding of the interior of the Cathedral and of its ultimate connection with the Bishop's House and the Choir School by means of cloisters. It will be noted that the Old Synod House (brick, with Ionic-columned portico) occupies the site of the South Transept.

**The Seven Ambulatory Chapels,** (see page 73 et seq.), may be identified on the exterior by the following characteristics (south to north): *Chapel of St. James,* rectangular plan, crenelated parapet of roof, and pinnacles on buttresses. *Chapel of St. Ambrose,* half round window arches. *Chapel of St. Martin of Tours,* fleurs de lis in quatrefoils above large windows; narrow pointed arch windows with single lights in basement. *Chapel of St. Saviour* (easternmost), rectangular plan; cross on gable; statues in niches of buttresses and wall. *Chapel of St. Columba,* angel on roof; statues in niches of buttresses. *Chapel of St. Boniface,* statues in niches of buttresses;

small mullioned windows of three lights in basement. *Chapel of St. Ansgarius,* rectangular plan; parapet of quatrefoil tracery; pinnacles on buttresses.

Three of the chapels have the following sculptures by Mr. Gutzon Borglum: *Chapel of St. Saviour:* On eastern wall above the great window, the Christ Child; in niches of buttresses on either side of window, Angels of the Resurrection; and beneath the window, the Virgin, seated between (left) St. Simeon who blessed the infant Jesus (Luke ii. 25-35) and (right) St. Zacharias, father of John the Baptist (Luke i. 67-80).* *Chapel of St. Columba:* On roof, an angel with hands joined in prayer; in upper part of great window, St. Columba with tamed wolf, recalling how be subdued wild beasts as well as wild tribes; and in niches of buttresses the four patron saints of the British Isles (left to right): St. David of Wales in beretta and fringed gown; St. George of England in armor with cross on shield and dragon at feet; St. Andrew of Scotland with diagonal cross†; and St. Patrick of Ireland, in Bishop's robes, with crozier in right hand and shamrock in left. *Chapel of St. Boniface:* In niches of buttresses, Charlemagne, with crown and sword; Alcuin, Charlemagne's preceptor, in monastic garb with manuscripts in right hand; Gutenberg, with book in each hand, his initials "J.G." on one; and Luther, in scholar's gown, with book between hands.

**The Clerestory of the Choir** rises above the roofs of the chapels. In the canopied niches near the top of the turrets and buttresses are 10 stone figures 9½ feet high by Mr. Borglum, as follows (south to north): St.

* The figures of the Virgin and the Child suggest the fact that the Chapel of St. Saviour occupies the position usually given to the Lady Chapel in European cathedrals.

† The diagonal cross of St. Andrew symbolizes not only the mode of his martyrdom but also humility. The legend is that when condemned to death, he asked to be nailed to a cross of a form different from the Saviour's as he was not worthy to die on the same kind.

James the Less with fuller's club (indicating manner of his martyrdom), and St. Philip with Latin cross (symbol of his crucifixion), together on turret; St. Bartholomew†; St. Thomas with square (spiritual architect); St. James the Great with staff (pilgrim); St. Peter with key (to the kingdom of Heaven); St. Andrew with diagonal cross; St. Matthew† with drapery over head; and St. Simeon with saw, and St. Jude with spear, (indicating manner of their death), together on turret.

**The Fourteen Stone Shields** which are located in the spandrels of the clerestory windows above the seven Ambulatory Chapels display the following devices, reading from south to north: Above Chapel of St. James, (left) winged ox; and (right) artist's palette, brushes and maulsticks, and lily, symbolizing St. Luke.* Above Chapel of St. Ambrose (left) lily, and (right) rose, both symbols of the Virgin Mary. Above Chapel of St. Martin of Tours, (left) eagle, and (right) chalice, symbols of St. John. Above Chapel of St. Saviour, (left) letters IC, XC, NI, KA,‡ in four quarters formed by a Greek cross, signifying Jesus Christ Conquers; and (right), initials SP, SF, SS, of the Latin words Sanctus Pater, Sanctus Filius, Sanctus Spiritus, (Holy Father, Holy

---

† The usual symbol of St. Bartholomew the knife with which he was flayed alive, and that of St. Matthew, the money bag, indicating his occupation before he was called, are not apparent.

* There is a tradition that St. Luke painted the first portrait of Christ. Pictures of the Madonna attributed to Luke are not uncommon in southern Italy. There is one such in the Cathedral of SS. Peter and Paul at Citta Vecchia, Malta. See article entitled "Knights and Sights of Malta" in Harper's Magazine for July, 1923, p. 159.

‡ IC and XC are the Greek letters iota sigma and chi sigma, (uncial form), being the first and last letters in each case of the Greek words for Jesus Christ. The letters NIKA are read together and spell the Greek word which means "conquers." Mrs. Jenner, in her "Christian Symbolism," says that this inscription "is stamped upon every altar-bread of the Orthodox Eastern Church, and it occurs on every eikon of our Lord."

Son, Holy Spirit), in a trefoil, symbolizing the Trinity. Above Chapel of St. Columba, (left) crossed keys, symbol of St. Peter, and (right) crossed swords, symbol of St. Paul. Above Chapel of St. Boniface, (left) winged lion; and (right) fig tree, both symbols of St. Mark. Above Chapel of St. Ansgarius, (left) winged man and (right) axe and book, both symbols of St. Matthew.

Surmounting the roof of the Choir, and facing eastward, is a bronze statue, 9½ feet high, by Mr. Borglum, representing St. Gabriel as Angel of the Resurrection, blowing a trumpet.

1. Jesus Christ Conquers. 2. Holy Father, Holy Son, Holy Spirit. 3 and 4. Saint Luke

## West Front

Returning to Amsterdam avenue and 112th street, we come to the main entrance to the Cathedral, and from the completed portion of the West Front can form an idea of the magnificent design in course of execution.* The first impression which one receives from the facade is that of its majestic proportions, its width, 207 feet, being several feet wider than the ordinary city block, and the two towers, 265 feet high, (named after St. Peter on the north and St. Paul on the south), having more than three times the height of the six-story houses across

* The West Front, which was begun May 6, 1925, and is now (November 15, 1928) up to the tops of the gables of the portals, is here described as complete.

THE WEST FRONT
(From Architect's Design)

the avenue. But its chief charm lies in its happy combination of vertical and horizontal features, the exquisite beauty of its details, and the originality with which its Gothic elements have been arranged. Some features suggest reminiscences of foreign cathedrals, but none is a copy. The facade, marked by the five portals and the five divisions formed by the buttresses, recalls the fronts of Bourges and Wells cathedrals, but it is different in proportions and details. Instead of the shallow porches of Bourges, we have here the depth of the porches of Rheims and Amiens, with their strong shadows, while the great verticals of Bourges and Wells are combined with the powerful horizontals of Paris and Amiens.

The first stage of the facade is occupied by the five portals, in and above which are blocks for the following statues, modeled by Mr. Lee Laurie and Mr. John Angel:

*North Tower Portal (Martyrs' Portal)*

On the left side going in, west to east: SS. Thomas a Becket, Catherine, Stephen, and Alban.

On the trumeau, or central door-post: St. Peter.

On the right side, west to east: SS. Denis, Joan of Arc, Vincent and Laurence.

On the gable: Archangel Michael.

*North Aisle Portal.*

Above the parapet: Moses.

*Central Portal (Portal of the Prophets)*

On the left side, west to east: Melchizedek, Abraham, Isaac, Joseph, Moses, and Samuel.

On the central door-post: Our Lord.

On the right side, west to east: David, Daniel, Isaiah, Jeremiah, Simeon and John the Baptist.

In the tympanum: A circular sculpture representing our Lord in Glory, surrounded by the Seven Lamps.

On the Gable: St. John the Evangelist.

*South Aisle Portal.*

Above the parapet: Elias.

*South Tower Portal (Preachers' Portal)*

On the left side, west to east: SS. Francis of Assisi, Bernard, Boniface and Chrysostom.

On the central door-post: St. Paul.

On the right side, west to east: SS. Dominick, Gregory, Patrick and Athanasius.

On the gable: Archangel Gabriel.

The second horizontal feature is an open gallery of small mullioned arches extending across the front above the porches.

The principal feature of the third stage is the great Rose Window, 40 feet in diameter. This is a characteristic of most Gothic cathedrals, but here is of a different design and is located at a relatively different height.

Next higher is another lovely arcade extending across the whole Front, in the position occupied by the Gallery of Kings at Rheims. (At Amiens and Paris the Gallery of Kings is below the Rose Window.) Above the central portion of the arcade project the gable of the Nave and two ornate buttress pinnacles.

Above this level, on the right and left hand, rise the belfries of the two towers, fifty feet square without spires but with pinnacles at the corners, following the examples of York and Canterbury rather than that of Paris.

In the buttresses at various heights are niches with statues, thus dispersing the figures which at Paris, Amiens and Rheims are concentrated in the Galleries of Kings.

## The Nave

Passing the massive bronze doors of the West Front and going through the narthex, or vestibule, one enters the Nave, and realizes more than ever the vast proportions of the Cathedral. As before stated, the "foundation stone" of the Nave was laid November 9, 1925. At present writing (November 15, 1928) the Nave is so nearly completed that it is here described as completed. The walls are up to the full height, and the vaulting and roof are finished. Some carving is yet to be done, the stained glass windows and chapel furnishings are not yet in place, and the mass of scaffolding has not yet been removed.

NAVE FOUNDATION STONE*

The seven stars and candlesticks (Rev. i. 20) are from the Cathedral Seal. The quotation is from I Cor. iii 11.

* The "foundation stone" is on the south side of the Nave in the first buttress east of the St. Paul tower. It contains the Bible, the Prayer Book, the Hymnal, copies of prayers by Bishop Manning for the building of the Cathedral, the Journal of the General Convention (1922), Journals of the Diocesan Conventions (1921 to 1925), a list of contributors to the Cathedral building fund, copies of the Diocesan Bulletin, daily newspapers of November 9, 1925, pamphlets relating to the campaign for building funds, a copy of the "Guide to the Cathedral Church of St. John the Divine," by Edward Hagaman Hall, L.H.D., and a printed copy of "The Cathedral: A Poem on the Building of the Cathedral Church of St. John the Divine" by the same author.

SOUTH SIDE OF THE NAVE, CROSSING AND CHOIR
(Photograph taken September 24, 1928)

Upon entering the Nave, which is 225 feet long, one has a clear vista eastward to the High Altar, a distance of about 500 feet (equivalent to about two city blocks), or about five sixths of the total length of the Cathedral, 601 feet. Looking upward, one has to tip the head backward 30 or 40 degrees to see the tops of the great arches 130 feet above the floor. And the breadth, 132 feet, gives room for five aisles, the central aisle being as wide between centers of piers as 112th street is between building lines.

Instead of the closely-grown-up forest effect produced by the columns of many Gothic cathedrals, an air of spaciousness is given by the relatively small number of piers and columns and their ingenious disposition. In this arrangement, the architect has made two notable departures from the ordinary Gothic type: One is the introduction of alternating slender columns in the primary line of piers, resolving the plan and the vaulting of the central aisle* into a system of four squares or double bays, instead of eight rectangular bays. The vaulting of each of these squares, however, is divided in two by a transverse rib springing from the smaller intermediate columns, thus producing, with the diagonal ribs of the square, a sexpartite vault,—the first and a unique example of its kind in America, and the loftiest ever attempted, according to the late Prof. A. D. F. Hamlin. The second innovation is the erection of the clerestory, not upon the primary lines of columns flanking the central aisle, but upon the secondary lines (those nearest the side walls), which produces two notable results: On the outside it modifies the system of flying buttresses; and on the inside it allows the piers and columns flanking the central aisle to rise without interruption from the floor to the spring of the great arches, producing an effect of soaring height and allowing, by the rhythmic alternation of large piers

* What is here informally called the central aisle is sometimes called by architects the Nave, to distinguish it from the parallel passages called aisles.

THREE BAYS OF INTERIOR OF THE NAVE

(Photograph from model. Human figures show scale. Height from floor to top of vaulting 130 feet.)

and relatively small columns, a play of light and shade surpassing that of any mediaeval cathedral.

Of the eight bays into which each wall aisle is divided, the bay nearest to the Crossing on each side is occupied by masonry, pierced by a door-way, leaving seven bays on each side to be illuminated by stained glass windows and to form little chapels. Each of these chapels is 25 feet wide, 18 feet deep and 43 feet high. Above the wall aisles runs the Triforium Gallery, and above the latter is the clerestory, with eight windows on each side. As the bays have been built by special groups of contributors, the chapel windows will be symbolical of the groups represented. Two bays have already been formally assigned, the easternmost bay on the north side to the *Historical and Patriotic Societies* (Dec. 11, 1927) and the westernmost bay on the same side to the *Sportsmen* (Jan. 29, 1928). In the westernmost bay on the south side will be the *Chapel of All Souls,* in which will be placed the *Golden Book* containing the names of all the donors to the building fund of the Cathedral. The arch over the middle aisle between the great piers nearest to the Crossing, built with gifts from children, is called the *Children's Arch;* and the pavement, representing contributions from visitors to the Cathedral, is called the *Pilgrim Pavement.*

The exterior walls of the Nave, as of other parts of the Cathedral, are of Golden Granite from the Mohegan Quarry near Peekskill, N. Y., while the inner walls are of Indiana limestone. The main piers of the central aisle, measuring 11 feet by 16 feet 3 inches, have an inner core of squared granite blocks weighing from 5½ to 7 tons apiece, faced with limestone; while the intermediate smaller columns are entirely of granite, each course being a single block weighing over 4 tons. The groin ribs are of cut stone, and the vaulting between the ribs is of two or more layers of Guastavino tiles. The facing tiles are of a gray color and are porous to absorb sound waves, and the superincumbent layers are of red tiles, laid in concrete, producing a monolithic structure. Above the vaulting, and invisible from below, is the only steel framework in the Cathedral, namely, the trusses supporting the roof. The roof, the ridge of which is 175 feet above the floor, is made successively of four inches of concrete, two inches of nailcrete, and heavy copper sheathing. Among the novel features of the structure are the snow-melting pipes laid in all gutters to promote the run-off from the roof into the conductor pipes during winter. Hidden in the floor and walls of the Cathedral, with a large proportion in the Nave, are about seven miles of conduits for electric wires and steam pipes. The sculptural work inside shows an almost endless variety of beauty and interest. In the capitals, no two of which are exactly alike, are carved various conventional symbols and many different kinds of animals and flowers.

## The Crossing

Walking through the Nave (2 on plan) we enter the Crossing (3), so-called from its location at the intersection of the long and short arms of the cruciform ground plan. In this space, 100 feet square, floored with concrete, are 1500 chairs for the congregation. To the eastward, the Crossing opens into the Choir (10) and Ambulatory (12-12). On the north and south sides the spaces between the ponderous piers of Maine granite are filled with temporary windows and concrete walls which will be removed when the North Transept and South Transept (4 and 5) are built. The rough, unadorned piers on the north, west and south sides will eventually be faced with Frontenac stone like those on the east side. The massiveness of this masonry may be judged by the fact that a single pair of these piers with connecting arch weighs 4,000 tons. The temporary *Dome* of the Crossing, 162 feet (just the height of Niagara Falls) above the floor, is a remarkable piece of construction, the tiles having been laid by the ingenious Guastavino method without the support of scaffolding.

**The Pulpit,** a memorial of Bishop Henry Codman Potter, is made of Knoxville, Tenn., marble, an uncrystalline limestone favorable for very fine work. On the newel posts of the stairs are the figures of the two great prophets of the Old and New Testaments, Isaiah (south) and John the Baptist (north). In the five principal Gothic niches are as many scenes in the life of Christ (north to south): The Nativity, Jesus Among the Doctors, the Crucifixion, the Resurrection and the Supper at Emmaus (Luke xxiv. 30-31). In the smaller niches are the figures of eight great exponents of the Holy Scriptures and champions of human freedom (north to south): St. Jerome, St. Gregory, St. Chrysostom, St. Peter, St. Paul, Hugh Latimer, Bossuet, and Bishop Phillips Brooks of Massachusetts.* Beneath these niches runs a moulding of grape-vine design symbolizing Christ the true vine† (John xv. 1) and beneath this one of roses symbolizing Christ the Rose of Sharon (Cant. ii. 1). On the base are the symbols of the four Evangelists: The winged man for St. Matthew, winged lion for St. Mark, winged ox for St. Luke, and eagle for St. John.‡ The pulpit is surmounted by a carved oak canopy of Gothic tracery, upon which is the beginning of the Gloria in Excelsis:

---

* These sculptures are surpassingly beautiful. The Supper at Emmaus has a particularly dramatic quality. Note the amazement of the two Disciples as they recognize the Saviour after his crucifixion, their attitudes and facial expressions, and the vein standing out on the neck of the one in the foreground.

† The use of the grape-vine to symbolize Christ dates from the very beginning of the Christian era. A silver chalice found in Antioch by Arabs in 1910 and believed to date from the 1st century, is covered with a grape-vine of twelve branches in the midst of which are figures of Christ and the writers of the Gospels and Epistles. (See N. Y. Evening Sun of Jan. 3, 1920, and N. Y. Times of May 14, 1922.)

‡ Concerning these symbols, see note on page 111.

THE PULPIT

"Glory be to God on high, and on earth peace, good will towards men. We praise thee, we bless thee, we worship thee, we glorify thee, we give thanks to thee for thy great glory. O Lord God, heavenly King."

On the side of the stairs is inscribed:

"In Memory of Henry Codman Potter. The gift of Mrs. Russell Sage. A. D. 1916."

The pulpit was designed by Mr. Henry Vaughan.

**The Litany Desk** at the eastern end of the middle aisle (often removed) is of carved oak. Surmounting the ends are two praying angels, while on the front are statues of St. Michael with sword, St. John with chalice, and St. Gabriel with lilies, all facing the Altar. An inscription reads:

"We beseech Thee to hear us Good Lord. Grant us Thy Peace. Have Mercy Upon us."

The desk was given by the Laymen's Club.

## The Central Tower

Over the Crossing will rise the Central Tower, 460 feet high. This tower has involved one of the most difficult problems presented to the architects, Messrs. Cram & Ferguson. The great size of the Crossing, 100 feet square inside and 126 feet square outside the main piers, was already determined by the location of the piers by the first architects, Messrs. Heins & La Farge. The latter intended to cover this space with a dome capped by a spire; but a dome presented many problems, engineering and artistic, and Messrs. Cram & Ferguson made several studies for a tower in its place. The magnitude of the problem will be better understood when it is recalled that the area of the Crossing, nearly 16,000 square feet, is more than three times that of the great octagon of Ely cathedral, and the extreme diameter, 126 feet, is 18 feet greater than that of the rotunda of St. Paul's in London. A square tower on such a base would have looked disproportionately large, especially when viewed diagonally. Tentative designs successively included a low square tower over the Crossing with two tall spires at the angles of the Nave and Transepts, an octagonal tower crowned with eight pinnacles, and a twelve-sided tower surmounted by a spire, but they were discarded. At last Dr. Cram has solved the problem ingeniously by the use of the secondary piers of the Crossing which are in line with the main arcades of the Nave and Transepts. By throwing two arches over the Crossing from the two northern secondary piers to the corresponding two southern piers, and similarly two arches from the eastern secondary piers to the corresponding western piers, he will produce by their intersections a support 60 feet square for a tower of that size hung over the 100-foot-square space beneath. (For further particulars, and illustrations, see the *Scientific American* of November, 1927.) The exterior effect of the four-square tower, with its different vertical planes and its stepped-in buttresses, culminating in four great and several lesser pinnacles, will be very beautiful and will be different from that of any other cathedral tower.*

## The Transepts

On the north and south sides of the Crossing are to be the two Transepts, each one as large as the Crossing. When they are finished, the present temporary walls will be removed, and the Cathedral at this point will be 325 feet wide. The North Transept, begun December 5, 1927, will be dedicated to the Virgin Mary and, quite appropriately, is being built by the contributions of women.

* In the article in the *Scientific American* of November, 1927, above mentioned, Mr. J. Bernard Walker, referring to the solid construction of the Cathedral of St. John the Divine, predicts that the Cathedral will stand for five thousand years, and gives his scientific reasons for his estimate.

The South Transept, not yet begun, will be dedicated to St. John the Evangelist.*

Approached from the outside, the facades of the two Transepts will present different but harmonious designs, the North Transept having only one deeply recessed portal, while its southern counterpart will have three. In the portals and on the buttresses there will be many statues. Both Transepts will have great Rose Windows, following the precedents of many French cathedrals. The strong vertical effect produced by the buttresses will be relieved on each Front by a horizontal arcade below the Rose Window and another above it. The Rose Window of the North Transept will be a memorial of Mrs. Hamilton R. Fairfax, first Chairman of the Women's Division of the Building Committee, who died in 1925.

The interior will follow the general scheme of the Nave, but in a simpler way, the Transepts having only three aisles instead of five, and the side aisles having only two bays each. The Triforium Gallery and the clerestory with its windows will form part of the series which, including those of the Nave, will eventually encircle the Cathedral. In one of the bays of the North Transept will be a shrine to the Virgin Mary, and in a bay of the South Transept one to St. John.

## The Choir

**Architecture.** The Choir (10) may best be surveyed from the eastern end of the Crossing. The half-round

---

* In the cruciform plan of the Cathedral, the North Transept corresponds to the right arm of the cross with reference to the person crucified, and the South Transept to the left arm. The dedication of these Transepts to the Blessed Virgin and St. John respectively follows a tradition of religious art dating from at least the ninth century which places St. Mary at our Saviour's right and St. John at his left as He hung on the cross, and recalls the tender chivalry of our Lord when, in his last moments, he commended his mother to the care of his Beloved Disciple. (John xix. 25-27.) See the sculpture of the Crucifixion on the front of the Pulpit.

THE INTERIOR OF THE CROSSING AND CHOIR

arches and other features exhibit a late Romanesque style with Byzantine influence, which is not inappropriate to the eastern end of the Cathedral, and which will become a relatively local detail as the prevailing Gothic style of the whole Cathedral develops.* The interior facing is of Frontenac stone. The broad course of red jasper from South Dakota seen at the base of the piers of the great Choir arch appears also in the Ambulatory (12-12-12) running entirely around the Choir. The green moulding above the jasper is Pennsylvania serpentine. The floor of the Choir has three principal levels. From the Crossing five steps lead to the Choir proper which contains the stalls and which occupies the first two bays. An ascent of six more steps leads to the second level which may be designated as the Presbytery. Upon it are the two thrones hereafter mentioned and the altar rail, the latter a step higher.† In the Sanctuary within the altar rail, 4 steps lead to the third level upon which stands the Altar with its 3 white steps.‡ Around the Sanctuary stand eight Great Columns described hereafter.

**The Parapet** at the entrance to the Choir is designed to represent outstanding characters of 20 centuries of the Christian Era. It is in two sections, one on each side of the steps leading from the Crossing to the Choir, each section being 18½ feet long and 4 feet high. It is built mainly of Champville (France) marble, in modified

* These Romanesque features are part of the original design which was subsequently abandoned. There is a plan for changing them to Gothic.

† There is much ambiguity in the use by architects of terms to indicate the sub-divisions of the eastern limb of a cathedral which is called comprehensively the Choir. The designations here used—the Choir proper, the Presbytery, and the Sanctuary—are sufficient for present purposes without confusing the reader with conflicting definitions.

‡ For details of intentional departures from absolute levels, and from regularity of height and spacing of arches, see "Temperamental Architecture" in "The New York Architect" for April, 1911.

French Gothic style. The twelve marble columns, alternately green, red and yellow, are of Alps Green from Italy, Rouge de Rance from Italy, and Numidian from Africa, respectively. The figures, from right to left, are as follows (authorities differing slightly as to some of the dates given): (1) St. Paul (died A. D. 66) with sword symbolizing his decapitation; (2) St. Justin Martyr (100-165) with axe and block; (3) St. Clement of Alexandria (150-220) holding cross in left hand; (4) St. Athanasius (296-373) pouring baptismal water from a sea-shell, referring to a playful incident of his boyhood which led to his calling; (5) St. Augustine of Hippo (354-430) with miter, pen and tablet; (6) St. Benedict (480-543) in habit of Benedictine monk pointing to scroll; (7) St. Gregory the Great (550-604) with slave child in broken shackles, referring to his intercession for pagan children in the slave market; (8) Charles Martel (688-741) with crown, battle-axe and pennant; (9) Charlemagne (742-814) with crown, scepter and orb; (10) Alfred the Great (849-901) crowned, with sword by side, holding three burnt cakes on book;* (11) Godfrey of Bouillon (1061-1100) crowned, with Crusader's sword and shield; (12) St. Bernard (1091-1153) in monk's habit, holding aloft a cross in his right hand and clasping a book in his left; (13) St. Francis of Assisi (1182-1226) in Franciscan monk's garb, contemplating a cross in left hand, and preaching to birds† in tree; (14)

---

* See Abbott's "History of King Alfred" for legends concerning the cakes. One is, that Alfred, when a fugitive from the Danes, was hiding one day in a peasant's cottage, and while sitting by the fireplace mending his bow, he was requested by the housewife to watch her cakes which were baking. Absorbed in thoughts of his kingdom, he forgot the cakes, and for his neglect was roundly scolded by the woman who little realized his character.

† St. Francis, founder of the Franciscan Order, literally interpreted the text "Go ye into all the world and preach the Gospel to every creature" (Mark xvi. 15) and a famous fresco by Giotto in the church of San Francesco, at Assisi, represents him preaching to the birds.

John Wyckliffe (1325-1384) with book and staff; (15) Columbus (1435-1506) lifting the veil from the globe, symbolizing the age of discovery; (16) Archbishop Cranmer (1489-1556) with right hand thrust voluntarily into the flame, symbolizing his martyrdom; (17) Shakespeare (1564-1616) standing amidst growing laurels; (18) Washington (1732-1799) in civilian attire as President; (19) Lincoln (1809-1865) standing by a burial cross delivering his Gettysburg Address; (20) uncarved block. The basis for selecting the figures was the representative character of the nineteen men selected in conjunction with their contribution to the development of Christian civilization. The Parapet was designed by Messrs. Cram & Ferguson, and the figures, modelled by Ferrari, were carved by John Evans & Co., of Boston. The Parapet bears the following inscription:

"To the Glory of God and in Memory of Richard Delafield, Brigadier-General, Chief of Engineers, Brevet Major-General, United States Army. Born September 1, 1798, Died November 5, 1873, This Parapet is Erected by his Children, Albert, Juliet Covington and Emma Delafield. Righteousness Exalteth a Nation: But Sin is a Reproach to any People."

**The Pavement.** The risers of the steps leading from the Crossing to the Choir are of yellow Numidian marble and the treads of green Pennsylvania marble. The pavement of the Choir, in Romanesque and Byzantine motives, is richly inlaid with Numidian, Swiss and other marbles and Grueby Faience tiles. The steps to the Presbytery are of marble from Hauteville, France. In the center of the floor of the Presbytery is a beautiful mosaic "rug" of tiles and marbles, 32½ feet long and 10 feet wide, with smaller patterns at the ends. In the center is an oval of black Belgian marble surrounded by violet marble from Italy, while Grueby tiles of many colors, and Grecian, red Numidian and other marbles form the rest of the design. The pavement of the

CHOIR STALLS

Sanctuary, within the communion rail, in addition to its designs of tiles and marbles, contains, immediately in front of the steps to the Altar, a red tile surrounded by a square brass border, inscribed:

**"Whoever shall have prayed at this spot will have pressed with his feet a tile from the ancient Church of St. John the Divine at Ephesus, built by the Emperor Justinian in the year DXL over the traditional site of St. John's grave."**

The tile was presented to the Cathedral by Bishop Kinsman of Delaware, its authenticity being attested by Prof. George Weber of Smyrna, who procured it from the ruins on the hill of Ayassolouk and who, in his lifetime, was a leading authority on Ephesian archaeology.

**The Eagle Lectern** of bronze at the north side of the Choir steps is a replica of an ancient lectern found near St. Albans Cathedral, England, in a lake into which it had been cast when that structure was destroyed in the Saxon invasion. The eagle, standing on a globe, is the symbol of St. John in his capacity as an Evangelist. Around the lectern are the figures of the four Evangelists: St. Matthew with open book, St. Mark with closed book and pen, St. Luke with open book in one hand and pen in other, and St. John with chalice. Below are their respective symbols. The lectern bears the following inscription, the initials at the end being those of the donor, Mary Gertrude Edson Aldrich:

"In Memoriam. Horatio Potter, Bishop of New York, 1854-1887. M. G. E. A."

**The Choir Stalls,** rising in four tiers on either side of the Choir proper, are of carved American oak. The canopies are after studies of those in the Chapel of Henry VII in Westminster Abbey used as the Chapel of the Knights of the Order of the Bath. The finials of the stalls are figures of great musicians and composers of church music, as follows:

*East.*

| *Left.* | *Right.* |
|---|---|
| Bortniansky | Mendelssohn |
| Handel | Haydn |
| Bach | Purcell |
| Tallis | Palestrina |
| Pope Gregory | St. Cecilia |
| Asaph | King David |

*West.*

The figures, modeled by Mr. Otto Jahnsen, are represented in the costumes of their day; and the features of all but those of David and his chief musician Asaph are from portraits.

The high canopied stall nearest the Crossing on the south side of the Choir is the *Dean's Stall.** It is a very skillful blending of styles to harmonize with the Jacobean canopies of the Choir Stalls and the Flamboyant note in the stalls themselves. It has many interesting details of carving, notably the three panels depicting the Good Shepherd (front), Learning (east side), and Charity (west side). On the back of the stall is inscribed:

"In the Name of the Father, Son & Holy Ghost. This Stall is Dedicated by The Head Mistresses Association to the Memory of Agnes Irwin. 1841-1914. Holding fast the faithful word as she had been taught, herself being not disobedient unto the heavenly vision. Head Mistress of the Agnes Irwin School, 1867-1894. First Dean of Radcliffe College, 1894-1909. First President of the Head Mistresses Association, 1911-1914."

In the Presbytery, on the south side, is the lofty *Bishop's Throne* of carved oak, while opposite to it is one with a little lower canopy for the use of a bishop other than the Diocesan.

* "Cathedral Choirs . . . have for ages been divided into two portions facing each other and respectively named Decani, or the side of the Dean, . . . and Cantoris, or the side of the Cantor" or Precentor.—Hunt's Concise History of Music.

On one of the Choir Stalls is inscribed:

"These Stalls are Erected to the Glory of God and in Loving Memory of Susan Watts Street. 1818-1893. By her Daughter, Anna L. Morton."

On a tablet in the Choir is inscribed:

"The Stalls of the Sanctuary and the Choir are Erected to the Glory of God and in Memory of Susan Watts Street. 1818-1893. By her Daughter, Anna Livingston Morton."

The ornate *Communion Rail* is of English oak. Its ten supports are in the form of narrow Gothic arches in which are as many figures of angels bearing censers, lyres, scrolls, etc. Upon the rail is the following inscription:

"To the Glory of God and in Loving Memory of Anna Livingston Morton. May 18, 1846-August 14, 1918. Given by her Daughter Edith Morton Eustis, 1920."

The *Screens in the Sanctuary* back of the sedilia are of oak in decorated Gothic style. On the middle panel of the northern (left) screen, behind the Bishop's seat, is the coat-of-arms of the Diocese of New York. The Screens were given in memory of George Macculloch Miller and his wife Elizabeth Hoffman Miller by their children and grandchildren.

**The Organ,** seen in the upper arches on either side of the Choir, contains 7,000 pipes and a chime, connected by electric wires with the console located in the gallery on the south choir screen. The console has four manuals and two octaves of pedals, 106 speaking stops, 31 couplers, and 33 pistons. A Gothic tablet in the south Ambulatory is inscribed:

"This Organ is Dedicated to the Praise of the Blessed Trinity and in Loving Memory of Lena Kearny Morton. 1875-1904. By her Parents, Levi Parsons Morton and Anna Livingston Morton."

THE HIGH ALTAR

The organ was built by the Ernest M. Skinner Co. of Boston. (See also Choir School, page 122.)

**The High Altar** is of white Vermont marble. The beautiful Gothic *Reredos* is of pierre de Lens, quarried in the vicinity of the city of that name in France. In the center is a majestic figure of Christ. On His left, (in order from center to spectator's right) are Isaiah, Jeremiah, Ezekiel and Moses, representing the Old Testament; and on His right (in order from center to spectator's left) are St. John, St. James, St. Peter and John the Baptist, representing the New Testament. The scale of the Cathedral may be judged from the proportions of the figure of our Saviour, which is seven feet high. Those of Moses and John the Baptist are 6 feet 10 inches high. In smaller niches on the front and sides are 16 angels holding various emblems— palm, sword, shield, swinging lamp, crown, trumpet, etc. Under the pedestals of the statues are clusters of grapes, symbolizing Him who gave His body and blood for man. The statue of Christ was made by Sig. Leo Lentelli under the direction of Mr. Carl Bitter. The other figures were modeled by Mr. Otto Jahnsen. The rectangular panel in the Reredos is filled with a very beautiful

Credence Table with Shaft made of Magna Charta Stones

Spanish embroidery in arabesque design, 200 years old. Upon the Altar is the following inscription:

"To the Glory of God and in Memory of Anna Livingston Morton. 1846-1918."

**The Credence Table,** at the right (south) side of the High Altar, is supported by a shaft composed of three stones from the ruins of the ancient Abbey of Bury St. Edmunds, England, in which the Barons met on November 20, 1214, and swore before the altar to secure from King John the liberties which they embodied in *Magna Charta*. These relics are of Caen stone, and may be recognized by their gray color. They were given to the Cathedral in 1922, with the consent of the Abbey authorities, by the Marquis of Bristol through Dr. Raphael Constantian of New York. Near the shaft is the following inscription:

"The Adjoining Shaft Was Once a Part of the High Altar of the Abbey of Bury St. Edmunds, Upon Which, on November 20, 1214, the Barons Swore Fealty to Each Other in Wresting the Great Charter from King John. It is Placed Here as a Symbol of the Community of Political Tradition, Laws and Liberties, Which is the Inheritance of the English Speaking Commonwealths Throughout the World."

**The Eight Great Columns** standing in a semi-circle around the Sanctuary and forming seven interspaces opposite the seven Ambulatory Chapels are among the marvels of the Cathedral. They are approached in size only by those in St. Isaac's Cathedral, Petrograd. The shafts of light gray granite from Bear Island, near Vinal Haven on the coast of Maine, were quarried as monoliths and turned on a specially constructed lathe. When the first two were subjected to the pressure of polishing they broke, and the contractor then obtained permission to make the shafts in two pieces. The lower stone in each shaft is 38 feet high and weighs 90 tons, and the upper stone is 17 feet high and weighs 40 tons, the total height between base and capital being 55 feet and the weight 130 tons. The octagonal capitals of pierre de Lens by Mr. Post represent singing angels. The columns were given as memorials of the men whose names are carved on the bases seen in the Ambulatory (south to north): "Alonzo Potter,* Bishop of Pennsylvania, 1800-1865"; "Colonel Richard Tylden Auchmuty, U. S. V., 1831-1893"; "Harry Manigault Morris, 1817-1892"; "Eugene Augustus Hoffman, 1829-1902"; "John Jacob Astor, 1763-1848"; "John Divine Jones, 1814-1895"; "Josiah Mason Fiske, 1823-1892"; and "Joseph Lawrence, 1788-1872."

**The Clerestory Windows** of the Choir, nine in number, of which seven are above the entrances to the seven Ambulatory Chapels, are designed to depict the Book of Revelation of St. John the Divine. Seven of them are in place. They are of painted mosaic glass made by Messrs. James Powell & Sons of London, Eng., according to thirteenth century methods. Each window is of three lights with rose window at the top, and is 28 feet high and 17 feet wide. The seven windows above the entrances to the seven Ambulatory Chapels (north to south) are designed to symbolize in their circular lights the messages to the seven churches in Asia mentioned in the Book of Revelation (i. 11), in the order there named: Ephesus, Smyrna, Pergamos, Thyatira, Sardis, Philadelphia and Laodicea. They are connected by the inscriptions in their lower borders which read consecutively as follows:

"Grace be unto you, and Peace, from Him Which is, and Which was, and Which is to come; From the Seven Spirits which are before His throne. Jesus Christ, the Faithful Witness, The First Begotten of the Dead, The Prince of the Kings of the Earth. To Him be Glory and Dominion for ever and ever"

---

* Brother of Horatio Potter and father of Henry Codman Potter, Bishops of New York.

SANCTUARY AND GREAT COLUMNS

These windows, which are of surpassing charm to the unaided eye, flash out with extraordinary brilliancy of color and affecting beauty of composition and execution, particularly those called "Christ Reigning in Glory" and "the Woman in the Sun," when examined with long distance glasses (apply to Verger), although the less brilliant windows contain subtle details well worth studying, as, for instance, the symbolisms of the elements held by the angels in the window above the Chapel of St. Boniface. Individually, from north to south:

**St. John and the Seven Churches** are the subject of the window above the *Chapel of St. Ansgarius.* In the upper part of the central light, St. John between two praying angels is depicted in the character of Apostle, beardless, and holding the sacramental cup—the young St. John, symbolical of love and high ideals and the feeling which filled all his writings; while in the lower part he appears as the aged exile on the Isle of Patmos, sitting with book in lap and pen in hand, listening to the angel behind him who commands him to write (Rev. i. 11). In the side lights are the angels of the seven churches (i. 11), bearing on scrolls their names: (Upper left) Ephesus; (lower left) Smyrna and Pergamos; (upper right) Thyatira and Sardis; (lower right) Philadelphia and Laodicea. In the circular light at the top are the name "Ephesus" and a shield bearing the seven candles mentioned in the message to the church of Ephesus (ii. 1). In the lower border of the three lights runs the inscription: "Grace be unto you, and Peace, from Him." The window was given by Mrs. E. C. Ludlow Johnson in memory of Gabriel Ludlow.

**The Natural Elements** upon which the vials of the wrath of God were poured (Rev. xvi. 2-17) are the principal subject of the window above the *Chapel of St. Boniface.* In the lower part of the left side light is an angel holding between his hands the earth (green foliage); in the middle light three angels respectively holding the air (invisible), the sun (yellow glow), and the sea (green waves); and in the right side light an angel holding the rivers and fountains (blue currents). In the upper part of the middle light is the Lamb that was slain (v. 12) between the four beasts (iv. 7) which are in the side lights—on the left, the lion and the beast with the face of a man; and on the right, the ox and the eagle.* In the circular light at the top are the word "Smyrna" and a shield bearing the crown of life mentioned in the message to the church in Smyrna (ii. 10). In the bottom border is the inscription: "Which is, and Which was, and Which is to come." A tablet in the Ambulatory reads as follows:

"The Clerestory Window Above the Chapel of Saint Boniface is Dedicated to the Glory of God and in Loving Memory of Annie Allen Wallace. February 14, 1853-August 25, 1890."

**The Seven Angels with Trumpets** (Rev. viii. 2) are the main subject of the window above the *Chapel of St. Columba.* Three of them are in the lower part of the middle light and two in each of the side lights. In the upper part of the middle light is the mighty angel of the cloud, overarched by the rainbow, standing upon the sea, and holding aloft in his left hand the little open book (x. 1, 2). In the upper part of the left side light is the angel with the seal of the living God (vii. 2) and in the right side light the angel with the golden censer (viii. 3). In the middle of the side lights are four angels (two left and two right) blowing the four winds of the earth (vii. 1). In the circular light at the top are the name "Pergamos" and a shield bearing the sharp two-edged sword of Him who sent the message to the church in Pergamos (ii. 12) between the Greek letters IHC and

* See reference to the symbols of the four Evangelists on page 111.

XPC (Jesus Christ).‡ In the bottom border are the words: "From the seven Spirits which are before His throne." A tablet in the Ambulatory reads as follows:

"The Clerestory Window Above the Chapel of Saint Columba is Erected to the Glory of God and in Loving Memory of—1797 John Williams Leeds 1873—1800 Eliza Leeds 1885—Emily Irene Hardenbergh 1899—By Their Daughter and Sister, Josephine Eliza Leeds, A. D. 1915."

**Christ Reigning in Glory,** as described in the first chapter of the Book of Revelation, is the principal subject of the great central window above the *Chapel of St. Saviour.* In the central light is the Son of Man, with up-raised hands, vested as King and Priest, wearing a royal crown, a crimson mantle and a golden pallium. He stands in the midst of the seven candlesticks (i. 13), holds in his right hand the seven stars (i. 16, 20), and is surrounded by winged seraphim. Beneath him a rainbow (iv. 3) over-arches the sea of glass (iv. 6). In the side lights are the four principal archangels: St. Michael (left, above), is depicted in armor as the Prince of the Celestial Armies, while the balance in his left hand, supposed to contain the souls of the dead, symbolizes his character as Guardian Angel of Departed Spirits. St. Raphael, below him, with pilgrim's staff, is represented as the friendly traveller, recalling Milton's "affable archangel." St. Gabriel (right, above), appears as Angel of the Annunciation, as indicated by the lilies (symbol of purity) in his right hand; and below him is St. Uriel, as Angel of Light, holding the sun. In the circular window at the top are two angels holding the morning star mentioned in the message to the church in Thyatira (ii. 28), but the name "Thyatira" is lacking. In the border at the bottom of the three lights are the words: "Jesus Christ the Faithful Witness." A tablet in the Ambulatory reads:

‡ See page 77 following.

"The East Window is Erected in Memory of Whitelaw Reid. October 27, 1837—December 15, 1912."

**The Seven Last Plagues** (Rev. xv. 1) are the principal subject of the window above the entrance to the *Chapel of St. Martin of Tours.* These are represented in the lower part of the window by seven angels holding the seven vials containing the plagues, three in the central light and two in each of the side lights. In the upper part of the middle light is an angel holding aloft in his right hand the everlasting Gospel (xiv. 6) in the form of a scroll bearing (obscurely) the symbols of the four Evangelists. In the upper part of the left side light is the angel with the measuring rod (xi. 1), and in the right side light is the angel standing in the sun (not to be confused with the woman in the sun mentioned in the next window), calling the fowls of the air to the supper of the great God (xix. 17). In the circular light at the top are the name "Sardis" and a shield bearing a white dove in the midst of the seven stars (the seven Spirits of God), mentioned in the message to the church in Sardis (iii. 1). In the border at the bottom of the three lights are the words: "The First Begotten of the Dead." A tablet in the Ambulatory reads:

"The Clerestory Window Above the Chapel of St. Martin of Tours is Erected to the Glory of God and in Loving Memory of Sophia R. C. Furniss and Mary B. Hubber, by Margaret E. Zimmerman, nee Furniss. Blessed are the peace-makers, for they shall be called the children of God."

**The Woman in the Sun** is the title of the window above the entrance to the *Chapel of St. Ambrose.* In the central light is the woman clothed with the sun and wearing the crown of twelve stars (Rev. xii. 1). She is surrounded by a dazzling radiance of flaming rays. Above her, a cloud of glory is carrying her Child up to the throne of God (xii. 5). In the left side light, above, is the angel proclaiming the fall of Babylon (xiv. 8), and below, symbolizing that wicked city, the woman in scarlet holding the golden cup of abominations and seated on the beast from the bottomless pit (xvii. 4, 18). In the right side light, above, is the angel with the sharp sickle and the clusters of the vine (xiv. 18), and below, the angel with the keys to the bottomless pit and the chain to bind the dragon (xx. 1). The whole window symbolizes the triumph of Christ over the forces of evil. In the circular light at the top are the name "Philadelphia" and a shield upon which, between six D's, is the key of David mentioned in the message to the church in Philadelphia (iii. 7). In the border at the bottom are the words: "The Prince of the Kings of the Earth." A tablet in the Ambulatory is inscribed:

"The Clerestory Window Above the Chapel of Saint Ambrose is Erected to the Glory of God and in Loving Memory of Morgan Lewis Livingston, 1800-1869, and Catharine Manning Livingston, 1810-1886, By Their Daughter Julia Livingston. 1916."

**The Heavenly City** is the principal subject of the window above the entrance to the *Chapel of St. James.* In the lower part of the middle light is the angel showing to St. John the Heavenly City (Rev. xxi. 10 et seq.) and in the upper part is a glorified figure symbolizing the holy city, new Jerusalem, coming down from God out of heaven prepared as a bride adorned for her husband (xxi. 2). Beneath this figure in the upper part is the pure river of water of life, and on either side of it is the tree of life whose leaves are for the healing of the nations (xxii. 1-2). In the lower part of the left-hand light is the angel with the Alpha, and in the corresponding part of the right-hand light is the angel with the Omega (xxii. 13); while above each of them is a beckoning angel saying "Come" (xxii. 17). In the circular light at the top are the name of the church of Laodicea and the word "Amen"— the latter being the name of the sender of the message to the Laodiceans (iii. 14) and the word with

THE BAPTISM OF CHRIST
16th century painting signed:
"Æredes Pavli Caliarii faciebant"

which the Book of Revelation and the Bible end (xxii. 21). In the bottom border of the three lights is the inscription: "To Him be Glory and Dominion for Ever and Ever."

## The Ambulatory

The Ambulatory (12-12-12) is a passage about 20 feet wide leading entirely around the Choir and giving access to the seven Chapels, Baptistry and Vestry Room. The pavement is of clay-red tiles with borders of grassy green serpentine and green marble from Pennsylvania. The beautifully colored wainscoting between the great pillars is of Grecian marble from the island of Scyrus. The Ambulatory is entered through elaborately wrought steel gateways, 30 feet high, in the archways on either side of the great arch of the Choir. The gates were presented by the Cathedral League and the Diocesan Auxiliary. In the south gateway is a white marble tablet, showing in relief two angels and two portrait medallions of Mr. and Mrs. Levi P. Morton, and bearing the following inscription:

**"To the Glory of God and in Enduring Memory of Levi Parsons Morton, 1824-1920, Vice-President of the United States, Governor of the State of New York, and of His Wife, Anna Livingston Morton, 1846-1918, Whose Gifts Made Possible the Building and the Furnishing of the Choir of this Cathedral. Yea saith the Spirit, that They May Rest from Their Labours, and Their Works do Follow Them."**

**A Notable Painting** from the atelier of the brother and sons of Paolo Caliari (Paul Veronese, 16th century) portraying the Baptism of Christ, hangs in the Ambulatory. It is signed in Latin with the firm name under which Paolo's associates continued business after his death: "The heirs of Paolo Caliari made it."

**The Founder's Tomb**, containing the remains of Bishop Horatio Potter, sixth Bishop of New York,* in the Ambulatory between the fourth and fifth great pillars opposite the entrance to St. Saviour's Chapel, is a beau-

THE FOUNDER'S TOMB

tiful example of an "altar tomb" such as are seen in many English churches. Its position, immediately behind the High Altar, is that traditionally reserved for the Founder of a cathedral. It is designed in the English Gothic style

* Uncle of Bishop Henry Codman Potter, seventh Bishop of New York, whose tomb is in the Chapel of St. James.

of the 15th century after studies of the tomb of Edward the Confessor in Westminster Abbey. The sarcophagus, the recumbent figure of the Bishop and the figures of the five ornamental niches of the front are of Indiana limestone. The figures, from left to right, are those of (1) Edward the Confessor, with crown, scepter and orb; (2) St. Remigius, with cup and scourge; (3) St. John the Divine, with pen, book and eagle; (4) St. Isidore, with miter, pallium and crozier; and (5) St. Theodosius of the Eastern Church, wearing a coronet with cross, holding a staff and reading from a scroll. Above the niches is a decorative moulding of oak leaves and acorns† with little squirrels at the ends. On the edge of the slab on which the Bishop's figure rests is inscribed:

**"Horatio Potter, D.D., D.C.L., Oxon. Sixth Bishop of New York, Founder of this Cathedral. Died 2d Jany. 1887, Aged 85 Yrs."**

On the rear of the sarcophagus is inscribed "St. John's Day ✠ Anno Domini 1921," the day on which the Bishop's remains were transferred from Poughkeepsie to this tomb. Above the tomb, reaching to a height of 15 feet above the pavement, is a canopy of American oak with richly carved frieze and cresting, supported on corbels springing from the great granite columns on either side. A narrow stairway behind the columns and the tomb leads to a landing which permits a closer view of the figure of Bishop Potter. The architect was Mr. Thomas Nash of New York and the sculptor of the figures was Mr. Isidore Konti of Yonkers, N. Y.

**The Brownell Memorial Tablet** on the wall of the bay at the entrance to the Chapel of St. Ansgarius reads as follows:

† The symbolism applicable to Bishop Potter's work is that of the familiar adage, "Great oaks from little acorns grow."

"In Memory of The Right Reverend Thomas Church Brownell, S.T.D., LL.D. Born 1779; Died 1865; Third Bishop of Connecticut, 1819-1865; Presiding Bishop, 1852-1865; and in Grateful Remembrance of the Foundation of the Bishop Brownell Memorial Fund for the Endowment of the Cathedral by His Daughter, Frances Johnston Holland."

Choir Boys' Stone

**The Choir Boys' Stone** on one of the piers of the Ambulatory near the Chapel of St. Ansgarius, is the bust of a boy of the class of 1911, carved by Mr. William Scott. It represents the choir boys' contribution to the building of the Cathedral. It contains, within a hollow, the names of the charter members of the Choir School and of the members of the class of 1911.

## The Seven Chapels of Tongues

The seven Chapels of Tongues, built around the Choir on lines converging toward the Sanctuary and deriving their name from the fact that they were intended for services of the church in the languages of the principal ethnological groups or regions of the world, are one of the noblest conceptions of the Cathedral. In early Gothic churches, the fundamental idea of the apse with radiating chapels was Christ in the company of his Saints. Here, in the great cosmopolitan Diocese of New York, this idea has appropriately been carried a step further in these chapels to include the idea of all the nations of the earth gathered around the Altar of the Saviour of Mankind. They recall the cry of the multitude in Jerusalem at Pentecost: "How hear we every man in our own tongue wherein we were born . . . the wonderful works of God" (Acts ii. 8, 11). Services in foreign languages are held in these chapels on special occasions, and have included services in the Armenian, Japanese, Chinese, Greek, Italian, Russian, Serbian, Spanish, Swedish and Welsh tongues. Services in English are held in one or more of the chapels every day of the year. As a group, the chapels eloquently express the catholic and democratic spirit of the Cathedral referred to on page 14. They may be visited in order either from south to north or from north to south, but by beginning on the south side they will be seen in the order in which they were observed on the exterior, and by looking through the archways of the Choir to the opposite side of the Ambulatory, glimpses may be had of the clerestory windows in the order in which they have been described. The chapels are all separate gifts and are memorials of the persons mentioned under their respective headings following:

## The Chapel of St. James

**St. James, the Apostle, after whom this chapel is named, was the son of Zebedee and was a Galilean fisherman. He is sometimes called St. James the Great to distinguish him from another Apostle called St. James the Less. He was a brother of St. John the Divine. He went almost everywhere with the Lord. After the ascension, he preached a while in Judea and then in Spain. After his mission there, he was beheaded by the Jews, and, according to tradition, his body was miraculously transported back to Spain, where his relics are said to rest at Compostella. Spanish historians chronicle 38 instances in which he is believed to have descended from heaven and in shining white armor led the Spanish armies against the Moors. Under the Spanish equivalent of his name, St. Iago or Santiago, he became the patron saint of Spain and his name was adopted as the Spanish war-cry. His shrine at Compostella was one of the most popular for pilgrimages in the Middle Ages, and it was said that two visits to Compostella equaled one to Rome. St. James is usually represented in the dress of a pilgrim with a peculiar staff. His Memorial Day is July 25.**

The Chapel of St. James (13 on plan), designed by Mr. Henry Vaughan, is in pure English Gothic *Archi-*

THE CHAPEL OF ST. JAMES

*tecture* of the 14th century; 66 feet long and 39 wide, with a sort of transept 15 feet wide. Its interior walls are of Bedford, Ind., limestone. On the front of the *Altar* of gray Knoxville, Tenn., marble, is sculptured DaVinci's Last Supper. The central feature of the limestone *Reredos* is a relief representing the Transfiguration, after Raphael. In four niches, two on either side of the Transfiguration, are statues of the four Evangelists with their appropriate emblems at their feet (left to right); St. Matthew with winged man; St. Mark with lion; St. Luke with ox; and St. John with eagle. Beneath the Transfiguration is a smaller sculpture of the Nativity, with an alleluia angel on each side. On four escutcheons, two on each side of the Nativity, are emblems of the condemnation and crucifixion (left to right); (1) Crown of thorns and spear (John xix. 2, 5, 34); (2) pillar to which Christ was bound for scourging, cord, knotted scourge (John xix. 1) and sponge on reed (John xix. 29); (3) ladder, sponge on reed and spear; and (4) hammer, pincers, coat, and three dice (Mark xv. 24). Beautifully carved canopies surmounted by six adoring angels crown the Reredos. The stained glass *East Window,* by C. E. Kempe & Co. of London, above the Reredos, depicts in its three lights (left to right) St. Lawrence, St. James and St. Vincent. In two walled-up panels of the window, one on each side of the glass, are statues of St. Peter with keys (left) and St. Paul with sword (right). *The Saint James Window* in the middle bay of the south aisle portrays in its four lights scenes in the life of the patron saint of Spain (see page 74) and other subjects, as follows, reading from left to right: Bottom, (1) Coat-of-arms of St. James and the words, "James, servant of God;" (2) St. James preaching to the natives of Spain; (3) St. James before the judge, forgiving his accuser and giving him his blessing, "Peace be with thee;" (4) Coat-of-arms of King Ramira I of Spain, and the words (to be read with those first quoted), "And of the Lord Jesus

Christ." Middle, (1) "Unto his shrine the mighty and the lowly fared on pilgrimage;" (2) "St. James, the radiant knight, upon a great white horse;" (3) "Before the banner of his name the Moorish warriors fled;" (4) "At Compostella still men serve Santiago's shrine." Top, (1) angel with IC-XC symbol; (2) "They bore his body to a ship that sailed for Spain;" (3) "Over his tomb they built a chapel passing fair;" (4) Angel with Ichthus symbol.* In the tracery at the extreme top is a representation of the Crucifixion. The window was given by Bishop Potter's daughters and was designed and made by Mr. Henry Wynd Young, glass-painter, of New York City. In niches of the walls of the chapel are the following statues and symbols: *East Wall,* St. Augustine of England with crozier (left) and St. Gregory the Great (who sent him to England) with papal tiara and papal cross (right). *West Wall,* end of main aisle, above, Christ between his kinsmen St. James the Great (left) and St. James the Less (right); and at end of south aisle, the Venerable Bede. On four escutcheons, two on each side of the west door, are: (1) A floriated cross (emblematic of the flowering or productiveness of the Christian religion); (2) the monogram ihc (representing the first two and last letters, uncial form, of the Greek word for Jesus†); (3) the Greek cross form of the chi rho monogram (first two Greek letters of the name Christ); and (4) the Alpha and Omega, the first and last letters of the Greek alphabet, (Rev. i. 8). *North Wall,* statue of William of Wykeham. In the upper

---

* Concerning the IC-XC symbol, see page 35.

† These letters **ihc** and the corresponding capitals IHC (iota, eta, sigma), are the first two and last letters of the Greek word for Jesus. They are frequently associated with the letters XPC (chi, rho, sigma), the first two and last letters of the word for Christ. When converted into the Roman form of **ihs** or IHS, they are sometimes construed to be the initials of the words Jesus Hominum Salvator (Jesus Saviour of Men).

part of the north wall is the gallery of the organ, which is independent of the great organ of the Cathedral. (See p. 58.) Two clustered columns divide the south aisle into three bays in the middle one of which is *Bishop Potter's Tomb* of Siena marble. On the tomb is a recumbent figure of the Bishop in Serevezza marble, by Mr. James E. Frazer. The Bishop is represented in his episcopal robes, and the execution is so fine that even the texture of the lawn sleeves is apparent. On the front of the tomb is inscribed:

Henry Codman Potter. MDCCCLXXXIII Assistant Bishop of New York MDCCCLXXXVII; Bishop of New York, MDCCCLXXXVII-MCMVIII. Upholder of Righteousness and Truth. Soldier and Servant of Jesus Christ."

On the rear:

"He laboured that this Cathedral Church Should rise to the Glory of God and as a witness to the Life of our Lord and Master Jesus Christ, that here the prayers of the chlidren of many lands should rise to that Father in whom alone all men are brothers, Whose service is perfect freedom."

Around the edge of the top slab:

"I saw the Holy City coming down from God out of Heaven, and I heard a great voice saying, Behold the tabernacle of God is with men and he will dwell with them and they shall be his people."

On the west wall is inscribed:

"The Chapel of St. James. Consecrated May 2, 1916, To the Worship of Almighty God, And in Loving Memory of Henry Codman Potter, Bishop of New York: Born May 25, 1834; Died July 21, 1908. The Gift of His Wife, Elizabeth Scriven Potter: Born September 30, 1848; Died March 4, 1909."

## The Chapel of St. Ambrose

St. Ambrose, or Ambrogio, the namesake of this chapel, was born in Treves about 340, the son of a Roman Prefect in Gaul (now France). While in his cradle one day, a swarm of bees settled upon him, clustering around his mouth, but doing him no harm. A similar thing having happened to Plato, it was

THE CHAPEL OF ST. AMBROSE

**considered an omen of future greatness. He studied law at Rome, became a magistrate in upper Italy with court at Milan, and by his wisdom and gentleness won such popular esteem that when called upon to settle the succession of the bishopric of Milan between the Arians and Catholics he himself was chosen by both parties to be Bishop of that see. He was one of the most celebrated fathers of the church. His most distinctive symbol is the beehive, although two human bones, the scourge, the crozier, the mitre, etc., are sometimes used. The Memorial Day for St. Ambrose is kept on April 4.**

The Chapel of St. Ambrose (14 on plan), designed by Messrs. Carrere & Hastings, is in modern Renaissance *Architecture*. It is about 50 feet long and 27 wide. The floor is inlaid with grey Siena, red Verona and cream-colored Cenere marbles. The side walls are lined with Rosato marble. On the under side of the marble archway at the entrance are reliefs representing the Three Persons of the Trinity with angels, as follows: (Left) the Father in human form*, with triangular nimbus, holding the globe of sovereignty; angel with lute; angel with lily; (top) the Holy Ghost in form of the dove; angel with trumpet; angel praying; and (right) the Son in form of the Paschal Lamb. The false perspective of the side walls is similar to that in the Sacristy of the Cathedral of Siena. In the spandrels of the false arches of the left-hand wall (as one faces the Altar) are figures in relief (reading from entrance toward Altar) of: Moses and the prophets, Isaiah, Jeremiah and Ezekiel; and on the opposite wall, in same order, St. Matthew with cherub, St. Mark with lion, St. Luke with ox, and St. John with eagle. The ceiling is artistically modeled in low relief. From the ceiling hang four silver lamps, one an antique Italian lamp and the others copied from

---

*** This rare representation of God the Father in human form is after examples developed during and confined almost entirely to the 14th-16th centuries. The triangular nimbus is peculiarly the symbol of God the Father. The Father is also represented in human form, seated on the throne, in the symbol of the Trinity in the lantern of the Baptistry, q. v.**

it. On the front of the *Altar* of alabaster are three golden ornaments, representing the Paschal Lamb (Christ) between two angels swinging censers, the latter symbolizing the prayers of all saints (Rev. viii. 3). The *Reredos,* not copied from any one European prototype but inspired by many examples found in the transitional and early Renaissance period in Italy, is of carved wood overlaid with gold leaf. The lower part consists of a triptych, covered by an elaborate canopy and flanked by niches in which are statues of St. Francis (left) and St. Ambrose (right). In niches at the left of the canopy are figures (left to right) of a kneeling angel, St. Benedict with crozier, St. Agnes in female apparel, and Dante in red gown and hood; and at the right (same order) Fra Angelico, Galileo with globe, Savonarola, and kneeling angel. Upon the cross of the canopy is a dove, symbolizing God the Holy Ghost; above that is the all-seeing eye in a triangle within a sun-burst, symbolizing God the Father; and on the top-most spire is the figure of God the Son holding a cross and pronouncing a benediction. *The Apse Windows,* one on each side of the Altar, transmit a soft amber light which gives a peculiar charm to this chapel. Each has a border of Italian Renaissance tracery, within which is a field of many small panes of leaded glass. In the *left window* these panes are ornamented with repeated designs representing the chalice with emerging serpent and the eagle (symbols of St. John), flowers, and the chi-rho monogram. In the upper part are the seven stars and candlesticks from the Cathedral seal, and the legend, "Sigil. Eccles. Cath. S. Johan;" and in the lower part the words, "For God is the King of all the Earth. Sing ye Praises with Understanding." In the *right window* the panes are ornamented with repetitions of the bee-hive, mitre and scourges (symbols of St. Ambrose), the cross and wreath, flowers, and the IC-XC and IHS symbols. Near the middle is a small fragment of brown glass, marked with an "R," from

Rheims Cathedral. In the upper part is the coat-of-arms of St. Ambrose—the bee-hive, mitre and croziers—with the legend, "Sigil. Sanct. Ambrosii," and in the lower part are the words, "God is our Refuge and Strength, a Very Present Help in Trouble." The windows were made by Mr. Henry Wynd Young, glass-painter, under the supervision of Messrs. Godwin & Sullivant, architects, of New York. Along the side walls are *Stalls and Wainscoting* of dark Italian walnut, inlaid with pear-wood in designs including the star of the east, chalice, Latin cross, patriarchal cross, and Bishop's mitre. Inlaid in the top border of the wainscoting is this inscription:

> (Left) "Holy, Holy, Holy, Lord God of Hosts. Heaven and earth are full of thy glory. Glory be to Thee, O Lord Most High. Blessed is he that cometh in the name of the Lord. Hosannah in the Highest. (Right) O Lamb of God, that takest away the sins of the world, grant us thy peace. Glory be to God on high, and on earth peace, good will towards men. Thou only, O Christ, with the Holy Ghost, art most high in the Glory of God the Father."

The ornate wrought iron *Screen* at the entrance to the chapel is best seen from the inside. Upon the finials at either end are angels blowing trumpets, and the space between them is divided by seven tall candlesticks into eight spaces, in which are bronze groups representing scenes in the life of St. Ambrose (left to right): (1) His youth; (2) settling the succession of the bishopric of Milan; (3) his baptism; (4) nuns and (5) monks, listening to the preaching of St. Ambrose, who stands between them facing the Altar; (6) the public penance before St. Ambrose of Emperor Theodosius who caused the massacre of the Thessalonians;* (7) laying the corner-stone of the Church of St. Ambrogio in Milan; and (8) his death. Beneath the figure of St. Ambrose who stands

* When Theodosius, in the year 390, caused the deliberate massacre of about 7,000 Thessalonians gathered in the circus, as punishment for lynching a brutal governor, Ambrose refused to admit the emperor to the sacrament until he publicly expressed his penitence before the whole congregation. Five years later the emperor expired in the arms of Ambrose.

THE CHAPEL OF ST. MARTIN OF TOURS

between the nuns and monks is a bee-hive with crossed croziers. On the south wall is inscribed:

"To the Glory of God and in Loving Memory of Augustus Whiting, Sarah Swan Whiting, Jane Whiting, Amelia Whiting Davis, Augustus Whiting, Jr., Natica Rives Burden, This Chapel has been Erected by Sara Whiting Rives."

## The Chapel of St. Martin of Tours

ST. MARTIN, after whom this chapel is named, born in 316, in his young manhood was a Roman soldier in Gaul. One wintry day, (according to the traditional story related by Ruskin in his "Bible of Amiens"), when Martin was riding forth from the city of Amiens, he saw a beggar shivering by the roadside; whereupon he divided his cloak with his sword and gave one half to the beggar. That night in a vision he saw Christ wearing the half cloak and surrounded by angels. And Christ said to the angels: "Know ye who hath thus arrayed me? My servant Martin, though yet unbaptized, hath done this." After this, Martin was baptized; but he remained a soldier for 17 years. Then, after several years of religious works, he was made Bishop of Tours. It is related that one day, when going to church in his full robes, he practically repeated the charitable act beforementioned by giving his stole to a ragged beggar; and when St. Martin was at the altar, elevating the Host, a globe of light appeared above him and angels descended and hung chains of gold and jewels (not of earth) on his bare arms. Sweet, serene and dearly beloved, he was Bishop and Knight of the Poor, and the divided cloak and sword are his special symbols. The Memorial Day for St. Martin is kept on November 11.

The Chapel of St. Martin of Tours (15 on plan), designed by Messrs. Cram & Ferguson, is in early 13th century Gothic *Architecture*. It is about the same size as the Chapel of St. Ambrose just described. Its interior walls are faced with light-colored Bedford, Ind., limestone. The lower half of the walls is occupied by Gothic arcatures, in the trefoiled arches of which are fleurs de lis. Under the fleurs de lis, in mediæval text, runs the inscription:

(Left side): "They that be wise shall shine as the brightness of the firmament and they that turn many to righteousness

JOAN OF ARC STATUE
In the Chapel of St. Martin of Tours

as the stars forever and ever. (Right side): The Peace of God which passeth all understanding shall keep your hearts and minds, through Christ Jesus."

A little above the arcature is a border of roses. The upper half of the side walls presents a unique feature in a sort of triforium gallery built in the thickness of the wall. The pavement of Knoxville, Tenn., pink marble is bordered with black Belgian marble. The simple marble *Altar* in the form of a table resting on red marble pillars has no reredos. The *Windows*, by Mr. Charles Connick of Boston, Mass., are of grisaille* work in geometrical designs, the Apse windows being inset with pictorial medallions in painted mosaic glass in the mediaeval style. In the central window over the Altar the medallions depict scenes in the life of St. Martin as follows, beginning at the bottom and reading upward: In the left-hand light (1) St. Martin receives sword and enters army; (2) divides his cloak with the beggar; (3) has vision of Christ wearing the severed cloak which he had given to the beggar; and (4) is baptized. In the middle light, (1) He converts the robber; (2) revives the dead man; (3) is affectionately welcomed on his return to Tours; and (4) destroys the heathen temple. In the right-hand light, (1) He intercedes with Count Avitianus for the release of prisoners; (2) pleads for Priscillian's life; (3) dies; and (4) the ship bearing his body is mysteriously propelled. In the middle light of the window at the left of the Altar are scenes in the life of St. Louis: (1) His coronation; (2) his release of prisoners at Paris; (3) his ministration to sick soldiers during the first Crusade; and (4) his departure on the second Crusade. In the middle light of the window at the right of the Altar are scenes in the life of Joan of

* Grisaille, from the French "gris" meaning "gray," so-called on account of the grizzled or grayish brown glass often employed. Windows in geometrical designs are also called pattern windows. Other examples of grisaille windows are those in St. Columba Chapel.

Arc: (1) Her vision; (2) the capture of Orleans; (3) the coronation of Charles VII.; and (4) her martyrdom at the stake. In the circular lights at the top of the seven windows are the following coats-of-arms (left to right): (1) On a blue field, three golden fleurs de lis above a white wreath of oak and laurel with red fruit, representing the City of Rheims.* (2) On a blue field sprinkled with golden fleurs de lis, the Mother and Child, representing the Cathedral of Notre Dame in Paris. (3) Seven horizontal bars, alternately blue and gold, being

Coats of Arms in Windows of Chapel of St. Martin of Tours.

the arms of Bertrand d'Eschaux, Archbishop of Tours. (4) On a blue field, a white Latin cross with trefoiled ends, being the arms of the Chapter of Poitiers. (5) On a blue cloak surrounded by red, a white sword, cross-hilt upward, emblematic of St. Martin. (6) On a blue field sprinkled with golden fleurs de lis, a red Greek cross,

---

* The designer has taken artistic license with these colors. Strictly, the arms of the City of Rheims are: On a silver field, a green wreath of oak and laurel with red fruit; on a blue chief three fleurs de lis of gold.

representing the Archdiocese of Rheims.† (7) On a blue field, three golden fleurs de lis under a white "label" or mark of cadency of eldest son, being the royal arms of the Dukes of Orleans.‡ A *Statue of Joan of Arc,* expressing her spiritual character, by Miss Anna Vaughn Hyatt, was placed in this chapel in 1922. It was given by Mr. J. Sanford Saltus through Dr. George F. Kunz, President of the Joan of Arc Statue Committee which erected the equestrian statue of the Maid by the same sculptress in Riverside Drive. Near it are two rough stones from the Chateau de Rouen in which the Maid was imprisoned at the time of her trial and from which she was led to the stake. The wrought-iron *Screen* of beautiful tracery at the entrance is a very lovely example of this form of art. While not copied from any existing mediæval prototype, it shows the influence of the wrought-iron work of the Romanesque and early Gothic periods of France. The shell ornament in the section below the cornice is symbolical of St. Martin as a pilgrim, while the finials and cresting, blossoming with roses, signify the flowering of the Christian religion. In the frieze are four panels depicting four scenes which are described in a quaintly lettered inscription in the moulding above:

> "S. Martin shares cloak with Beggar. Our Lord appears in cloak to S. Martin. S. Martin receives holy baptism. Saint Martin journeys to Rome."

An inscription on the wall of the chapel reads:

> "The Chapel of Saint Martin of Tours. Consecrated 1918 To the worship of Almighty God and in Loving Memory of William P. Furniss and His Wife Sophia Furniss and their Daughter Sophia R. C. Furniss."

---

† Strictly, the arms of the Archbishop of Rheims are: On a blue field sprinkled with golden fleurs de lis, a silver cross over all.

‡ In 1376, Charles V. fixed the number of fleurs de lis in the royal arms at three "to symbolize the Holy Trinity." Some persons consider that the three leaves of the conventional fleur de lis also symbolize the Trinity.

THE CHAPEL OF ST. SAVIOUR

In another panel is this inscription:

"To the Glory of God and in Loving Memory of Clementina Furniss, by Whose Gift this Chapel was Erected, and Margaret Elizabeth Zimmerman, Daughters of William P. Furniss and his wife Sophia Furniss."

In a small niche in the wall near the sacristy door is an iron cross called the *Lafayette Cross,* under which is the following inscription:

"To the Glory of God and as an Emblem of the Friendship between France and America this Cross, which was given by the Marquis de Lafayette on his last visit to America to the brothers of General Nathanael Greene of Potowomut, Rhode Island, is donated to the Cathedral of St. John the Divine by Richard Ward Greene Welling, 1928."

## The Chapel of St. Saviour

SAINT SAVIOUR, the name of this chapel, means Holy Saviour, the word Saint being used in its primary sense as an adjective, derived from the Latin "sanctus." The Memorial Day for St. Saviour is kept on the feast of the Transfiguration, August 6.

The Chapel of St. Saviour (16 on plan) forms the eastern end of the Cathedral. It is in the English Decorated Gothic style of *Architecture* after designs by Messrs. Heins & LaFarge. It is 56 feet long and 30½ feet wide. It was consecrated on April 19, 1911. Its interior walls are of Minnesota dolomite, around the base of which runs a foundation course of red jasper with green serpentine moulding like those which run around the Choir. The pavement is of stone from Hauteville, France, with a mosaic border. The steps to the Sanctuary are of pink marble from Georgia. The *Altar* is of snow-white Carrara marble. Its face and front corners are adorned by the figures of six angels singing "Holy, Holy, Holy." Carved on the face of the retable is the crown of thorns, supported by two cherubs. The *Reredos* is of polished red

Siena marble, bordered with Venetian mosaic. The *Chair and Prayer Desk* of black walnut at the left side of the Sanctuary have an interesting history recited on a brass tablet on the desk as follows:

"The first use of this chair and prayer desk was made by the Most Reverend Randall Thomas Davidson, D.D., Archbishop of Canterbury, in the Crypt of the Cathedral of St. John the Divine on Wednesday morning, September 28th, A. D. 1904, at the celebration of the Holy Communion, at which His Grace was the celebrant and which preceded the opening of the One hundred and twenty-first Convention of the Diocese of New York, being also the first opening of the Diocesan Synod Hall."

The *East Window,* a glorious work in stained glass by Mr. Hardman of Birmingham, Eng., completely fills the end of the chapel. Its central light is occupied by a representation of the Transfiguration (Mat. xvii. 1-3). In the middle of the scene is the radiant Saviour, with Moses (left) holding the Ten Commandments, and Elias (right) holding the receptacle of the scrolls, representing respectively the Law and the Prophets.* Surrounding the group are angels; and below it are the three Disciples who were with Jesus on the mount: St. Peter (left) looking up, St. James (middle) covering his eyes, and St. John, the beardless Disciple (right), shading his face. In the left side light, above, is Moses putting off his shoes on the holy ground before the burning bush from which the angel of the Lord appears (Ex. iii. 5); and below, Moses raising the brazen serpent for healing (Num. xxi. 9). The serpent, seen indistinctly coiled around the pole, is by artistic license represented in green. In the right side light, above, is the angel appearing to Elijah (I. Kings xix. 5-8); and below, Elijah's sacrifice miraculously consumed by the fire of the Lord (I. Kings

---

* This representation of the Transfiguration, like that in the reredos of the Chapel of Saint James described on page 76, is after Raphael's last work, the original of which is in the Vatican. In both cases the poses of the six figures have been adapted to the spaces occupied.

xviii. 30-38). In niches on either side of the window are the following *Statues* of Bishops, saints and scholars of the Eastern church:

| *Left.* | *Right.* |
|---|---|
| St. Polycarp<br>b. 69 d. 155<br>Bishop of Smyrna | St. Chrysostom<br>b. 347 d. 407<br>Archbp. of Constantinople |
| St. Athanasius<br>b. 296 d. 373<br>Primate of Egypt | St. Basil<br>b. 329 d. 379<br>Bishop of Caesarea |
| Origen<br>b. 185 d. 253<br>Great eastern scholar | St. Clement of Alexandria<br>b. circ. 150 d. 213-220<br>Celebrated Church Father |
| St. Gregory Nazianzen<br>b. 330 d. 389<br>Bishop of Nazianzus | St. Ignatius<br>b. circ. 50 d. 107<br>Bishop of Antioch |

In a niche in the upper part of the north wall is a statue of St. Peter with key; and in a corresponding niche in the south wall one of St. Paul with sword. Turning toward the entrance to the chapel, one sees in niches between the clustered columns at the sides of the great archway an array of angels, five on each side, one above the other, corresponding to as many on the Ambulatory side,— twenty in all — representing the Heavenly Choir. These lovely figures are worthy of more than passing notice. All the statuary is by Mr. Gutzon Borglum. The four *Lamp Standards* of Carrara marble surmounted by alabaster bowls standing in the corners of the chapel are carved in relief with many symbolical details. The elaborate wrought-iron *Screen* at the entrance, is in the Italian style after one in Orvieto, Italy. It is embellished in its upper part by two golden angels holding a wreath at the foot of the cross. Looking outward through the screen, one sees the back of the High Altar of the Cathedral. On one of the walls of the chapel is inscribed:

THE CHAPEL OF ST. COLUMBA

"This Chapel is Erected to the Glory of God and in Loving Memory of Bessie Morgan Belmont, by her Husband, August Belmont."

## The Chapel of St. Columba

ST. COLUMBA was born in County Donegal, Ireland, in 521, of royal blood. After study and religious work in Ireland, he set out in 563 with twelve disciples and planted upon the Island of Iona, on the west coast of Scotland, which he received from his kinsman Conal, King of Scots, a monastery which, from the 6th to the 8th centuries, was second to hardly any other in Great Britain. From it was conducted a wonderful missionary work in Scotland, Ireland, the north of England, and small adjacent islands. Many miracles are attributed to him, and he was accredited with power to subdue not only wild tribes of men but also the beasts of the wilderness (see p. 34). He died in 597, and his body was buried at Iona, which is regarded as one of the great shrines of Christianity in Great Britain. The Memorial Day for St. Columba is kept on June 9.

The Chapel of St. Columba (17 on plan), designed by Messrs. Heins & LaFarge in the Norman style of *Architecture,* is 50 feet long and 27 wide. The interior walls are of Minnesota dolomite, separated from a base course of Mohegan granite by a moulding of yellow Verona marble. The pavement is a fine grained gray stone from Illinois. The semi-circular arched window heads, and particularly the six large cylindrical pillars diversified by spiral and diaper patterns, convey the idea of the Norman style which one sees exemplified on a larger scale in Durham Cathedral and other churches of that period in England. The vaulting over the *Sanctuary* is lined with gold mosaic, upon which are Celtic crosses. The lectern shows a composition of three figures: Christ in the center, between John the Baptist, his Forerunner, and St. John the Divine, namesake of the Cathedral, who closes the biblical record with the Book of Revelation. The *Altar,* of cream colored Italian marble, is in the form of a table supported by marble pillars.

It has no Reredos. The three stained glass *Windows* were made by Messrs. Clayton & Bell of London. In the central light of the window above the Altar is represented the baptism of Christ by John the Baptist, and in the side lights are St. John with cup (left), and St. Paul with sword, (right). In the bottom of the three lights are the four symbols previously explained (p. 77), namely, the IHC, the Alpha, the Omega, and the Chi Rho. The windows on either side of the middle window are in grisaille, copied from the famous lancet windows called the Five Sisters in the North Transept of York Cathedral, although these windows have only two lights each, instead of five. The six wonderfully graceful seven-branched *Candelabra,* after Donatello, were brought from Italy by Mr. George Gordon King. Turning toward the entrance, in which is a wrought iron *Screen* in the Spanish style, one sees an extremely interesting feature in the *Statues* by Mr. Gutzon Borglum of representatives of the successive stages of the development of Christianity in England, which stand in the niches between the clustered columns at the sides of the great entrance archway.*

The figures, five on each side, one above the other, and corresponding to as many on the Ambulatory side,—twenty in all,—are in the following relative positions, it being understood that the left side as seen from the chapel is the same as the right side as seen from the Ambulatory.

---

* In the following table *ac.* indicates date of accession to title. Some of the dates here and on page 92 are only approximate.

*Seen from Chapel.*

| *Left.* | *Right.* |
|---|---|
| St. Aidan<br>Bishop of Northumbrians<br>ac. 635 d. 651 | St. Augustine<br>Archbishop of Canterbury<br>ac. 597 d. 604 |
| St. Anselm<br>Archbishop of Canterbury<br>ac. 1093 d. 1109 | King Alfred<br>King of Wessex<br>b. 849 d. 901 |
| Thomas Cranmer<br>Archbishop of Canterbury<br>b. 1489 d. 1556 | William of Wykeham<br>Bishop of Winchester<br>ac. 1367 d. 1405 |
| Joseph Butler<br>Bishop of Durham<br>b. 1692 d. 1752 | Jeremy Taylor<br>Bishop of 3 Irish sees<br>b. 1613 d. 1667 |
| John Keble<br>leader in Oxford movement<br>b. 1792 d. 1866 | Reginald Heber<br>Bishop of Calcutta<br>b. 1783 d. 1826 |

*Seen from Ambulatory.*

| *Left.* | *Right.* |
|---|---|
| St. Alban<br>promartyr of Britain<br>d. circ. 304 | Theodore of Tarsus<br>Archbishop of Canterbury<br>ac. 668 d. 690 |
| The Venerable Bede<br>chronicler and priest<br>b. 673 d. 735 | Stephen Langton<br>Archbishop of Canterbury<br>b. 1150 d. 1228 |
| John Wyckliffe<br>morning-star of Reformation<br>b. 1325 d. 1384 | Matthew Parker<br>Archbishop of Canterbury<br>b. 1504 d. 1575 |
| Richard Hooker<br>Anglican theologian<br>b. 1554 d. 1600 | George Berkeley<br>Bishop of Cloyne, etc.<br>b. 1684 d. 1753 |
| John Wesley<br>evangelical revivalist<br>b. 1703 d. 1791 | Frederic Denison Maurice<br>preacher and leader<br>b. 1805 d. 1872 |

The Cathedral has in its possession a *Stone from the Cathedral, or Church of St. Mary* (dating from the 13th-16th centuries) *on the Island of Iona,* which may fittingly be placed in this chapel at some future time.

THE CHAPEL OF ST. BONIFACE

Upon the wall of the chapel is inscribed:

"Chapel of Saint Columba. To the Glory of God and in Loving Memory of Mary Leroy King. The Gift of Her Mother, Mary Augusta King. Consecrated April 27th, 1911."

## The Chapel of St. Boniface

ST. BONIFACE, whose original name was Winifred, was born in Devonshire, England, about the year 680. He entered a Benedictine monastery at the age of 13, learned rhetoric, history and theology, and became a priest at the age of 30. At a time when England and Ireland were sending missionaries to the heathen parts of Europe, Winifred was authorized by Pope Gregory II. to preach the Gospel to the tribes of Germany, and he is called the Apostle of Germany. While engaged in this work, Gregory made him a Bishop and gave him the name of Bonifacius, or Boniface, which means Doer of Good. The Bishoprics of Ratisbon, Erfurt, Paderborn, Wurzburg, Eichstadt, Salzburg, and several others, owe their establishment to his efforts. In 746 he was made Archbishop of Mainz. In 755, while carrying on his work in Dokkum, in West Friesland, he and his congregation of converts there were slain by a mob of armed heathen. His remains are buried in the famous abbey of Fulda, which he founded. In art, he is depicted holding a book pierced by a sword, referring to the manner of his death. The Memorial Day for St. Boniface is kept on June 5.

The Chapel of St. Boniface (18 on plan), designed by Mr. Henry Vaughan, is a pure specimen of English Gothic *Architecture* of the 14th century. It is about 48½ feet long and 28 wide. The interior walls are of Indiana limestone; the pavement of pink marble from Knoxville, Tenn., with heavy black border of Belgian marble; and the steps to the Sanctuary also of pink Knoxville marble. The *Altar* is of gray marble from the same source. In the three ornate panels on its face are the monogram IHS (see p. 77), the floriated Greek cross (see page 99), and the Greek cross form of the Chi Rho (p. 77). The richly carved *Reredos* has three canopied niches, in the central one of which is represented the Adoration of the Magi. In each of the side niches is an angel with scroll. In the recesses of the windows on either side of the Altar are carved clergy stalls of dark oak, with wainscoting of the same wood as high as the window sills. There are six stained glass *Windows,* each with three lights. In the middle light of the central window above the Altar Christ is represented as the Great Teacher. His robe is sprinkled with the ihc monogram (p. 77) and in His nimbus appear the ends of a floriated cross.* Above His head are two angels, and above them the dove, symbolizing the Holy Spirit. Below the figure of Christ is a scene representing Him teaching the multitude. In the left side light is St. Boniface with mitre, archiepiscopal staff,† and Bible pierced with sword; and below him a scene representing him hewing down an oak in Geismar accounted sacred by the idolators. In the right side light is St. Paul with sword; and below him a scene representing him preaching to the men of Athens. In the left hand window of the Apse are three figures with scenes below as follows (left to right): St. Birinus, Bishop of Dorchester, holding a monstrance, and (below) St. Birinus baptizing King Cynegils of the West Saxons; St. Augustine of Canterbury with archiepiscopal staff, holding a tablet representing the crucifixion, and (below) St. Augustine announcing the Word of Life to King Ethelbert; and St. Felix, Bishop of Dunwich, with crozier and torch, and (below) St. Felix receiving the

---

* Only the nimbus of the Deity is ornamented with the cross. In a front view, but three arms of the cross appear; and sometimes these are represented as rays of light. A few writers, including G. J. French and W. & G. Audsley, contend that the three rays on the nimbus of the Deity have no connection with the cross, but symbolize the Trinity. The similarity of the floriated terminals to the French fleur de lis has no special meaning, the real significance being, as stated on page 77, the flowering or productiveness of the Christian religion.

† A Bishop's crozier is usually in the form of a pastoral staff, or ornate shepherd's crook; an Archbishop's staff has a cross instead of a crook at the upper end; and a papal staff has a double cross at the upper end. See description of Bishop Manning's crozier on page 25.

blessing of the Archbishop of Canterbury. In the right hand window, similarly, are: St. Chad, Bishop of Lichfield, holding crozier and model of Lichfield Cathedral,‡ and (below) St. Chad listening to the songs of angels; St. Columba in monastic garb with crozier and with monastery (Iona) at his feet, and (below) St. Columba converting the Picts; and St. Aidan with crozier, and (below) St. Aidan instructing the youthful St. Chad and others. In the western small window are: St. Patrick with crozier ornamented with shamrocks; St. Gregory of Rome with papal staff, holding an open music book displaying the Sursum Corda (referring to him as founder of the Gregorian music), with Pere Marquette below; and St. Martin of Tours with crozier and Bible. In the eastern wall are two small windows. In the left hand window of the two are: St. Cyprian, Archbishop of Carthage, holding his staff and his best known book concerning Church Unity, or the universal church; St. Ambrose, Bishop of Milan, with crozier and open book displaying the words "Te Deum Laudamus" (we praise Thee, O God), and pen in hand, with the missionary Robert Hunt below; and St. Augustine, Bishop of Hippo Mundia, with crozier. In the right hand window of the two in the east wall are: St. Cyril, Patriarch of Alexandria, with book and staff; St. John Chrysostom, Bishop of Constantinople, with staff, chalice and Book of Homilies, with the missionary John Robinson below; and St. Ignatius, Bishop of Antioch, holding a palm. The windows were made by Messrs. C. E. Kempe & Co. of London. In two canopied niches in the west wall are *Statues* of Thomas a Becket (left) and St. Boniface (right); and in a niche in the east wall is one of Erasmus. Three wrought iron *Lamps* are suspended by iron chains from the ceiling; and at the entrance is a handsome wrought iron *Screen* adorned with

‡ The founder of a see is usually represented holding the model of a cathedral.

THE CHAPEL OF ST. ANSGARIUS

escutcheons bearing the ihc monogram and surmounted by a floriated cross before explained. On one of the walls is inscribed:

"The Chapel of St. Boniface. Consecrated February 29, 1916. Erected to the Glory of God by George Sullivan Bowdoin and His Wife, Julia Grinnell Bowdoin, and Their Children, Temple Bowdoin, Fanny Hamilton Kingsford, Edith Grinnell Bowdoin."

## The Chapel of St. Ansgarius

ST. ANSGARIUS, or St. Ansgar, was born in Picardy in 801. With his co-laborer Autbert he went to preach Christianity to the northmen of Sleswick. In spite of much persecution, he was so successful that in 831 the Pope established an archbishopric in Hamburg, (afterwards transferred to Bremen), and Ansgarius was appointed first Archbishop. He made several missionary tours in Denmark, Sweden and other parts of the north, and died at Bremen in 865. He is called the Apostle of the North. The Memorial Day for St. Ansgarius is kept on February 3.

The Chapel of St. Ansgarius (19 on plan), designed by Mr. Henry Vaughan, architect of the Chapel of St. James, is in the same style of *Architecture,* 14th century Gothic, and about the same size, being 66 feet long and 41 wide. It differs, however, from the Chapel of St. James in plan, the bay east of the turret stairs being here thrown into the Ambulatory, while in the Chapel of St. James it is included as a sort of transept; and the north side of the Chapel of St. Ansgarius being divided into only two bays, while the south side of the Chapel of St. James is divided into three.

The interior walls are of Indiana limestone; and the pavement of pink Knoxville, Tenn., marble and mottled Vermont marble. The *Altar* is of gray Knoxville marble. On its front is carved the Madonna of the Chair, on the left of which, from the spectator's standpoint, is St. Michael with sword and on the right St. Gabriel with lilies. In the middle of the sculptured *Reredos,* (above) is represented Christ holding the globe (symbol of sovereignty), and (below) the baptism of Christ by John the Baptist.

On the left of the figures are St. Ansgarius with crozier (above) and Gustavus Adolphus with sword (below), while on the right are St. Olaf with crown and scepter (above) and Luther in gown with book (below). The Altar and Reredos were given by Mrs. Julia Grinnell Bowdoin. In the left (northern) wall of the Sanctuary is a niche made of *stones from Worcester and Ely Cathedrals,* England. On the upper surface of the stone bracket forming the shelf of the niche is carved "Ely 1320." The stones from the Lady Chapel of Worcester Cathedral were given to the Cathedral of St. John the Divine by Canon George William Douglas of New York who procured them from Canon J. M. Wilson, Archdeacon of Worcester.* On the stones on either side of the recess is carved:

"These Stones from the Cathedral of Christ and St. Mary the Virgin, Worcester, England, are Memorials to William Reed Huntington, Sometime Rector of All Saints in Worcester, Massachusetts."

Three small *Windows* of two lights each in the Sanctuary contain (from left to right) representations of: (1) St. Willibrod with mitre, archiepiscopal staff, and model of cathedral; and St. Lucian with crown, scepter and sword; (2) St. Ansgarius with mitre and crozier; and King Olaf with crown and scepter; and (3) above the Reredos, St. Eric with crown and scepter; and St.

* Some years ago, when Canon Douglas was visiting Worcester Cathedral, England, Canon Wilson pointed to a spot in the wall where an ancient carved stone had been replaced by a modern stone, and said: "A good while ago a man of the name of Huntington, who introduced himself as Rector of a church in Worcester, Mass., begged me to give him a bit of carved stone as a symbol of the ties between England and America." This led Canon Douglas to ask for a similar gift to be placed in St. Ansgarius' Chapel, which is a memorial of Dr. Huntington, in a House of God where Englishmen and Americans often meet and where members of the Daughter Church have constant occasion to recall their indebtedness to the Mother Church of England.

Wilifred with mitre and archiepiscopal staff. The window spaces at the right of the latter are walled up because they are blanketed by the adjacent chapel. In the two bays of the north aisle are two noble stained glass windows, each having five lights and each light depicting two scenes. In the left hand or western window, the upper tier of scenes is chiefly devoted to Old Testament subjects as follows (left to right): Adam and Eve (Gen. ii. 7-25); the visit of the three angels to Abraham bearing the promise of the birth of Isaac (Gen. xviii. 2-22); St. Michael fighting the dragon with a cross-shaped spear (Rev. xii. 7); Abraham offering to sacrifice Isaac (Gen. xxii. 9-13); and Jacob's dream of the ladder (Gen. xxviii. 12). In the lower tier are five scenes prophetic of the birth of the Forerunner of Christ and of Christ himself: The angel's visit to Zacharias to foretell the birth of John the Baptist (Luke i. 13); the annunciation to the Virgin Mary of the coming birth of Christ (Luke i. 28); St. Gabriel with lilies as Angel of the Annunciation (Luke i. 28); the angels' visit to the shepherds (Luke ii. 8-12); and the angel's visit to Joseph, husband of Mary, to foretell the birth of Christ (Mat. i. 20). The right hand or eastern window depicts Acts of the Apostles. In its upper tier are: St. Peter preaching to the Disciples (Acts i. 15); St. Peter healing the lame man (Acts iii. 2-8); St. Peter with key; the stoning of St. Stephen (Acts vii. 59); and St. Philip baptizing the eunuch (Acts viii. 26-38); and in the lower tier: St. Peter raising Tabitha (Acts ix. 40); the conversion of St. Paul's jailer at Philippi (Acts xvi. 23-31); St. Paul with sword; St. Paul laying hands on the Disciples (Acts xix. 6); and St. Paul before Felix (Acts xxiv. 24-25). All the windows are by Messrs. C. E. Kempe & Co. of London. In two high niches in the south wall are *Statues* of Eric, King of Sweden (left) and Canute, King of the English, Danes and Norwegians (right); and in a niche at the west end of the north aisle is

THE SACRIFICE

the figure of Archbishop Eskiel. On the Ambulatory side of the entrance bay are two statues: John the Baptist (above) and St. Ansgarius with crozier and mitre, holding a small cathedral (below). The sculptures are by Mr. John Evans of Boston. In a bay of the chapel temporarily rests a symbolic group executed in Caen stone by Miss Malvina Hoffman of New York, entitled *The Sacrifice*. It is intended for Harvard University at Cambridge, Mass., as a memorial of Robert Bacon, sometime U. S. Ambassador to France and a Trustee of the University, and of the Harvard men who lost their lives in the World War. It represents a dead Crusader, such as those who went from Cambridge, Eng., in the 12th century, and gave their lives for an ideal, lying upon a cross with his head pillowed in a woman's lap. According to the traditional position of the feet of the Crusader, he was one of those who never reached Jerusalem, those who did so being traditionally represented with their feet crossed. The woman may typify Alma Mater as well as those women who gave their best to a great cause and made their lonely grief their glory. The two figures symbolize mutual sacrifice. This chapel has an independent *Organ* played from a movable console on the floor. On one of the walls is inscribed:

"The Chapel of Saint Ansgarius. Consecrated April 3, 1918, to the Worship of Almighty God and in Loving Memory of William Reed Huntington, for 25 Years Rector of Grace Church, and for 22 Years Trustee of this Cathedral."

**The Corner Stone** of the Cathedral, which was laid by Bishop Henry C. Potter on St. John's Day, December 27, 1892, is imbedded in the northwestern pier of the Chapel of St. Ansgarius and is only partly visible in the chamber under the chapel. It is a block of gray Quincy granite, 4 feet 4 inches square and 2 feet 4½ inches thick. Upon the angle of the visible corner are inscribed a Greek cross and "I. H. S. St.

John's Day, Decem. XXVII, A. D. 1892." It contains, among other things, a fragment of a *Spanish Brick* from Hispaniola (Hayti) which was given to the Cathedral by Mr. Malcolm McLean, Senior Warden of St. Andrew's Church, New York City, and upon which is a silver plate inscribed:

"From the Ruin of the First Christian Church in the New World where the First Church was Erected by Christopher Columbus, 1493. Isabella, Hispaniola."*

## The Baptistry

The Baptistry is situated between the Ambulatory on the south, the Chapel of St. Ansgarius on the east, the Chapter House (not begun) on the north, and the North Transept (now in course of construction) on the west; and the only part of it visible from the outside is the lantern with its finial. It was begun on Ascension Day, 1924, and was consecrated by Bishop Manning on the Sunday after Easter, April 15, 1928. On the latter occasion the Bishop said: "In the opinion of those best qualified to judge, it ranks among the most beautiful baptistries in the world, and in our land there is no other to compare with it."

* The Corner Stone also contains a Bible, a Prayer Book, a Hymnal, Journals of the Diocesan Conventions 1882-1892, Journals of the General Conventions 1889-1892, Centennial History of the Diocese of New York, several church periodicals, three different almanacs for 1893, Catalogue of the General Theological Seminary and St. Stephen's College 1892-1893, New York daily papers of December 27, 1892, the form of service for laying the Corner Stone, names of the Cathedral Trustees, several charges and addresses delivered by Bishop Potter on various occasions, letters from the Bishop to the clergy and others concerning the Cathedral, the badge and rules of prayer of the Brotherhood of St. Andrew, medal of the Missionary Society, lists of principal officers of the United States, N. Y. State and N. Y. City governments, and a list of the objects placed in the stone.

The principal approach to the Baptistry is through a bay of the Ambulatory, forming a vestibule called the *Entrance Way,* which is an individual unit of the composition. It is separated from the Ambulatory by a beautiful bronze screen designed in the spirit of the typical reja, or grille, of the Spanish Renaissance. Upon the screen, over the gate-way, is the sentence: "Behold the Lamb of God which taketh away the sins of the world;" and at the left, lower down: "We bless thy holy name for thy servant Catherine E. S. Stuyvesant, Departed this life in thy faith and fear, 1924." Over the great archway leading into the Baptistry is the coat-of-arms of the Netherlands, flanked by statues of St. Nicholas on the right and St. Catherine on the left (see note on page 111). Under the figure of St. Nicholas is his symbol, the three roundels, or balls, representing the three purses which he gave to the poor nobleman for his daughters; and under that of St. Catherine is her symbol, the bladed wheel, recalling her torture. On the east wall of the entrance way is a statue of Judith Bayard, wife of Peter Stuyvesant, and under it is a bust of Augustus Van Horne Stuyvesant, father of the donors, as a child; and on the west wall is the figure of Louise Coligny, wife of William of Orange, under which is a bust of Harriet Le Roy Stuyvesant, mother of the donors, as a child. On the wall is carved the following inscription:

> "This entrance way to the Baptistry is erected to the glory of God and in memory of Catherine E. S. Stuyvesant by her sister and brother A. D. 1926."

Passing through the great archway into the Baptistry proper, one observes that the Baptistry is octagonal in plan, following the form frequently used for baptistries in European countries, notably those of Ravenna, Pisa, Florence and Gerona. The *Architecture* is 14th Century Gothic, showing both French and Spanish influence in its detail. The design was principally inspired by the cim-

THE BAPTISTRY

borio, or lantern, over the Saragossa Cathedral, but the characteristic Spanish, or Plateresque, detail of the Saragossa example has been eliminated and a more French type of detail used for moulding and ornament. The interior walls are of Indiana limestone. The Baptistry has a vaulted dome and octagonal lantern, and its principal interior dimensions are as follows: Diameter, 31 feet; height to the spring of the great vault, 26 feet; height to apex of vault, or beginning of lantern, 43 feet; and height to keystone of vault of lantern, 57 feet. The height from floor to top of finial over the lantern is 80 feet. From the interior of the Baptistry three doorways, other than the Ambulatory entrance, lead to the Chapel of St. Ansgarius, the Chapter House and the North Transept. The lower parts of the walls between the four doors are relieved by ornamental arcades. In a spandrel of the arcade on the northeast wall is the coat-of-arms of Stuyvesant, and above it is inscribed:

> "This Baptistry is erected to the glory of God and in loving memory of Augustus Van Horne Stuyvesant and Harriet LeRoy Stuyvesant by their children, Catherine E. S. Stuyvesant, Augustus Van Horne Stuyvesant, Jr., and Anne W. Stuyvesant. Dedicated Anno Domini MCMXXVIII."

Running around the Baptistry is a wide *Frieze* of sculpture illuminated in polychrome. In this frieze are eight statues in niches, flanked by sixteen shields supported by figures of angels. The shields bear the symbols of the Twelve Apostles and four other saints displayed heraldically. Above each shield is an open book. The books above the symbols of the Twelve Apostles are inscribed with the portions of the Creed attributed to them respectively, and the other four have appropriate quotations. Following is a list of the statues and symbols* beginning on the east side and reading to the right:

---

* The characters represented by the *Statues* recall the history of the Netherlands under whose auspices New Netherland (now New York) was settled. Stuyvesant was the last Governor-General of New Nether-

| *Symbols* | *Statues* | *Symbols* |
|---|---|---|
| Keys<br>St. Peter<br>Matt. xvi. 19 | Bishop Compton<br>See note<br>below | Eagle<br>St. John<br>See note |
| Scallop Shells<br>St. James<br>See note | St. Willibrod<br>Apostle of Frisians<br>658-739 | Diagonal Cross<br>St. Andrew<br>See note |
| Basket of loaves<br>St. Philip<br>John vi. 5-13 | Thomas a Kempis<br>Ascetic scholar<br>1379-1471 | Spears<br>St. Thomas<br>See note |
| Knives<br>St. Bartholomew<br>See note | Erasmus<br>Scholar and teacher<br>1467-1536 | Angel<br>St. Matthew<br>See note |
| Fuller's Bats<br>St. James Minor<br>See note | Grotius<br>Jurist and scholar<br>1583-1645 | Fishes<br>St. Simon<br>See note |
| Ship<br>St. Jude<br>See note | William of Orange<br>Netherlands Liberator<br>1533-1584 | Axes<br>St. Matthias<br>See note |
| Swords<br>St. Paul<br>See note | Henry Hudson<br>Navigator and explorer<br>Died 1611 | Tongues of Fire<br>St. Barnabas<br>Acts xi. 22-24 |
| Lion<br>St. Mark<br>See note | Peter Stuyvesant<br>Gov. New Netherland<br>1602-1682 | Ox<br>St. Luke<br>See note |

On the cornice of the frieze is the inscription:

---

land and an ancestor of the donors of the Baptistry. Hudson was an Englishman, but sailed under a Dutch commission when he explored the Hudson river. Compton, Lord Bishop of London, was named first Rector of Trinity Parish, New York City, in a charter granted by William III., formerly Prince of Orange. Supplementing the references in the text to *Symbols:* The symbols of the four Evangelists, supposed to be derived from Revelation iv. 7, and Ezekiel i. 10, are variously interpreted. One explanation of each is: The angel (messenger) is given to Matthew in his character of Evangelist; the lion to Mark, historian of the resurrection, because ancient naturalists believed the lion was born inanimate and came to life three days after birth; the ox, emblem of sacrifice, to Luke, because he dwells on the priesthood of Christ; and the eagle to John, because he soared in the spirit and saw God. The scallop shells represent James as the pilgrim by sea. Tradition says that Andrew chose the diagonal cross for his crucifixion; Thomas was killed by a spear: Bartholomew was flayed alive; James the Less was struck down by a fuller's bat; the head of Matthias was cloven by an axe; and Paul was decapitated by the sword. In many Anglican churches the fish is used to symbolize Simon, apparently in the belief that he was a fisherman; and works of art frequently associate a ship with Jude, for some reason not clearly apparent.

"Go ye, therefore, and teach all nations, baptizing them in the name of the Father, and of the Son, and of the Holy Ghost; teaching them to observe all things whatsoever I have commanded you. And lo, I am with you alway, even unto the end of the world."

In the heads of the great arches of the north, east, south and west walls are four rose windows; and in the corresponding spaces of the four alternate arches are circular medallions of ornamental stone tracery having at their centers the symbols of the four Evangelists. At the intersections of the ribs of the vaulted dome are sixteen *Bosses*. The eight in the inner circle represent scenes in the life of Christ: Isaiah's Prophecy, the Annunciation, the Nativity, the Flight into Egypt, the Baptism, the Last Supper, the Crucifixion, and the Ascension. The eight in the outer circle symbolize the gifts of the Holy Spirit. One (the seven doves) represents the Seven Gifts collectively, and the others represent in detail Wisdom, Understanding, Counsel, Ghostly Strength, Knowledge, Godliness, and Fear. Within the inner circle is the opening of the *Lantern,* 11 feet in diameter. The lantern is illuminated by eight Gothic windows, and in its top is a sculpture representing the Father and Son enthroned, and the Holy Ghost. In the smaller details of the Baptistry appear lilies and thorns interwoven, tulips and windmills suggestive of the Netherlands, the letter "S" standing for Stuyvesant, and many other symbols.

In the center of the Baptistry, raised three steps above the floor, is the *Font,* a monumental structure of Champville marble, about 15 feet high. It is octagonal in plan, conforming with that of the Baptistry, and in general form is similar to the one in the Lower Church of St. John the Baptist in the Cathedral of Siena; but it is treated in the Gothic instead of the Renaissance style. On its front are eight sculptured panels representing scenes relating to the life of John the Baptist. At the

THE FONT

right of each panel is the figure of an angel symbolical of the scene depicted. Beginning on the south side and reading to the left, the figures and scenes are as follows: (1) Angel of the Annunciation with lily: Heavenly messenger prophesying to Zacharias the birth of John (Luke i. 11-13); (2) Angel of Sorrow with cross, symbolical of Jesus and John: Visitation of the Virgin Mary to Elisabeth (mother of John) and Mary uttering the Magnificat (Luke i. 39-55); (3) Recording angel, with pen and ink: Zacharias naming the infant John (Luke i. 59-63); (4) Guardian angel praying: John in the Wilderness called to preach and baptize (Luke iii. 2-3); (5) Angel of Sacrifice with palm: John preaching (Luke iii. 3 et seq.); (6) Angel of Baptism with shell: John baptizing Christ in the Jordan (Mark i. 9); (7) Angel of Testimony with scroll: Christ testifying John's mission (Luke vii. 24-28); (8) Angel of Death hooded: John's martyrdom (Mark vi. 17-28.) At the top of the panels is a sculptured border representing, in alternate segments, water lilies symbolical of the Baptist, and roses symbolical of Jesus.

From the center of the bowl rises an octagonal pinnacled shaft. On the lower part of it are the coats-of-arms of the City of New York, the Diocese of New York, the Cathedral, and the donors. Higher, in four niches, are figures of the four Evangelists. On the buttresses flanking the niches are four adoring angels, one playing an instrument, one singing, one bearing a censer, and one praying. Still higher are eight figures symbolical of the Joyful and Sorrowful Mysteries: the Annunciation with lily, the Nativity with star, the Baptism with shell, the Last Supper with chalice, the Crucifixion with crown of thorns, the Crucifixion with three nails, the Crucifixion with Gloria and I. H. S., and the Ascension with ascending dove. Above all, surmounting the finial, is the figure of our Lord as a youth.

Upon the edge of the bowl is inscribed:

"To the glory of God and in loving memory of Augustus Van Horne Stuyvesant and Harriet Le Roy Stuyvesant this font is erected by their children ✠ One Lord, one Faith, one Baptism."

The Baptistry was designed by Messrs. Cram & Ferguson. The statues in the frieze and the bust of Augustus Van Horne Stuyvesant were modeled by Mr. John Angel; the sculpture of the font by Mr. Albert H. Atkins; the large figures in the vestibule by Messrs. W. F. Ross & Co.; and the bust of Harriet LeRoy Stuyvesant by Randolph Rogers (about 80 years ago).

## The Crypt

The Crypt, located beneath the Choir, is closed, pending the completion of other parts of the Cathedral. In it the first services in the Cathedral were held from January 8, 1899, until the Choir and Crossing were opened on April 19, 1911. It contains the tombs of the Very Rev. William M. Grosvenor, D.D., Dean of the Cathedral, who died December 9, 1916; the Right Rev. David H. Greer, eighth Bishop of New York, who died May 19, 1919; and the Right Rev. Charles S. Burch, D.D., ninth Bishop of New York, who died December 20, 1920.

---

*"Thou meeting-place of men and God sublime,*
*May thy firm walls endure for endless time.*
*To children's children without ceasing take*
*Thy blessed ministry of grace; and make*
*Each generation better than the last,*
*Till sin and sorrow here be overpast,*
*Lost Paradise on Earth be new begun,*
*And Earth and Heaven eternally be one."*

## Comparative Dimensions

Following are the principal dimensions of the Cathedral. As cathedrals are compared in size by their areas, the Cathedral of St. John the Divine will be the largest in any English-speaking country and the fourth largest in the world.

*Area*

| | |
|---|---|
| Area of Cathedral | 109,082 square feet |

*Length*

| | | |
|---|---|---|
| Western Towers | 50 | feet |
| Nave | 225 | " |
| Crossing | 100 | " |
| Choir | 170 | " |
| St. Saviour's Chapel | 56 | " |
| Total length | 601 | " |

*Width*

| | | |
|---|---|---|
| West Front (including buttresses) | 207 | feet |
| Nave and Aisles (exterior) | 132 | " |
| Transepts | 315 | " |
| Crossing | 100 | " |
| Choir | 56 | " |
| Ambulatory | 20 | " |

*Height*

| | | |
|---|---|---|
| Western Towers | 265 | feet |
| Ridge of Nave Roof | 175 | " |
| Nave Vaults (above floor) | 130 | " |
| Choir Vaults (above floor) | 127 | " |
| Crossing Vault (above floor) | 200 | " |
| Central Tower | 460 | " |
| Top of Tower above tide-water | 591 | " |

Following are the principal dimensions of 18 great cathedrals. The area is given in square feet and other measurements in linear feet. The exterior height is that of dome, tower or spire.

| *Cathedral** | *Area* | *Height Exterior* | *Height Interior* | *Length Exterior* |
|---|---|---|---|---|
| St. Peter, Rome............... | 227,069 | 448 | 150 | 718 |
| Virgin of the Assumption, Cordova ..................... | 167,113 | 300 | 38 | 443 |
| Mary of the Chair, Seville..... | 128,570 | 400 | 150 | 430 |
| St. John the Divine, New York. | 109,082 | 460 | 130 | 601 |
| Nativity of Mary, Milan...... | 107,000 | 355 | 153 | 500 |
| Christ, Liverpool ............. | 101,000 | 308 | 173 | 619 |
| St. Peter, Cologne............. | 91,464 | 512 | 145 | 511 |
| Notre Dame, Amiens.......... | 71,208 | 361 | 140 | 521 |
| SS. Peter and Paul, Washington | 71,000 | 262 | 95 | 534 |
| Agia Sophia, Constantinople... | 70,000 | 185 | 184 | 350 |
| Notre Dame, Chartres......... | 68,260 | 378 | 122 | 507 |
| Notre Dame, Paris............ | 64,108 | 204 | 110 | 390 |
| York Minster (St. Peter)...... | 63,800 | 198 | 99 | 486 |
| St. Paul, London.............. | 59,700 | 363 | 89 | 460 |
| St. Patrick, New York......... | 57,768 | 339 | 112 | 332 |
| Holy Trinity, Winchester...... | 53,480 | ... | 78 | 556 |
| Notre Dame, Rheims.......... | 48,985 | 270 | 124 | 483 |
| Westminster Abbey (St. Peter). | 46,000 | 225 | 101 | 511 |

**Symbols of St. Paul and St. Barnabas in the Baptistry Frieze**

* Seville Cathedral is dedicated to "Maria de la Sede." On the facade of the Duomo, at Milan, is inscribed "Mariae Nascenti." York Minster is "the Cathedral and Metropolitan Church of St. Peter in York." Westminster Abbey is "the Collegiate Church of St. Peter at Westminster."

## Bishops of New York

Following is a list of the Bishops of New York since the erection of the Diocese:

*First:* The Right Rev. Samuel Provoost, D.D.; born February 24, 1742; Bishop of New York 1787-1815; died September 6, 1815.

*Second:* The Right Rev. Benjamin Moore; born November 5, 1748; Assistant Bishop 1801-1815; Bishop of New York 1815-1816; died February 29, 1816.

*Third:* The Right Rev. John Henry Hobart, D.D.; born September 14, 1775; Assistant Bishop 1811-1816; Bishop of New York 1816-1830; died September 12, 1830.

*Fourth:* The Right Rev. Benjamin Tredwell Onderdonk; born July 15, 1791; Bishop of New York, active 1830-1845, inactive 1845-1861; died April 30, 1861.

*Fifth:* The Right Rev. Jonathan Mayhew Wainwright, D.D., D.C.L.; born February 24, 1792; Provisional Bishop 1852-1854; died September 21, 1854.

*Sixth:* The Right Rev. Horatio Potter, D.D., D.C.L., Oxon.; born February 9, 1802; Provisional Bishop 1854-1861; Bishop of New York 1861-1887; died January 2, 1887.

*Seventh:* The Right Rev. Henry Codman Potter, D.D., LL.D.; born May 25, 1834; Assistant Bishop 1883-1887; Bishop of New York 1887-1908; died July 21, 1908.

*Eighth:* The Right Rev. David Hummell Greer, D.D., S.T.D., LL.D.; born March 20, 1844; Bishop Coadjutor 1904-1908; Bishop of New York 1908-1919; died May 19, 1919.

*Ninth:* The Right Rev. Charles Sumner Burch, D.D., L.H.D., LL.D.; born June 30, 1855; Bishop Suffragan

1911-1919; Bishop of New York 1919-1920; died December 20, 1920.

*Tenth:* The Right Rev. William Thomas Manning, D.D., D.C.L., LL.D.; born May 12, 1866. Bishop of New York 1921.

THE BISHOP'S THRONE

# Part Three

# Other Buildings, Etc.

## The Bishop's House

The Bishop's House (A. on plan), is in French Gothic architecture of the chateau type, with lofty roof and high dormer windows, and is built of Germantown micaceous schist. It is designed to be connected with the Cathedral by cloisters, and is connected with the Deanery by a porch above which will be the Bishop's private chapel. The architects were Messrs. Cram & Ferguson.* The occupants of the house have been Bishop Greer from the time of its opening in 1914 until his death May 19, 1919; Bishop Burch from his installation October 28, 1919, until his death December 20, 1920; and Bishop Manning since his consecration on May 11, 1921.

## The Deanery

The Deanery (B. on plan) adjoins the Bishop's House as above mentioned. It is by the same architect, is in the same style but of a more domestic type, forms a part of the same architectural composition, and is built of the same kind of stone. It is not so lofty a structure as the Bishop's House, but has many interesting details, more particularly on the southern facade. The late Dean Grosvenor occupied the Deanery from the time of its erection until his death December 9, 1916, and was

* For details, see description in the Architectural Record for August, 1914.

THE BISHOP'S HOUSE

succeeded by Dean Robbins in June, 1917. A tablet in the porch is inscribed:

**"The Deanery. Erected in Faithful Remembrance of Clinton Ogilvie, 1838-1900, by his wife, Helen Slade Ogilvie. A. D. 1913."**

## The Choir School

The Choir School was founded by Bishop H. C. Potter in 1901 and was formerly located in the Old Synod House. The present building (C on plan), erected in 1912 and built of the same kind of stone as the Bishop's House and Deanery, is in the English Collegiate Gothic style of architecture. Messrs. Walter Cook and Winthrop A. Welch were the architects. Accommodations are provided for 40 resident scholars. Their musical training is under the personal direction of the Master of the Choristers, and their general education is under the direction of the Head Master and staff of assistant masters. A House Mother looks out for the personal wants of the boys and directs the domestic service. Boys are admitted to the school at the age of 9 and remain until their voices change, which is usually between the ages of 13 and 14. They come from all parts of the United States and possessions, two boys having come from Alaska. An applicant is first received on probation, and if he manifests a good character and disposition, and gives promise of a good voice, he is accepted as a chorister. During their residence at the school the boys are under strict discipline and have the finest education and musical training that can be given them. Their education and musical training are free but there is a charge of $250 a year for board and laundry. The men of the choir, of whom there are about 20, do not reside at the Choir School. The usual number of choristers, men and boys, in the Cathedral services is about 60, except during the summer vacation when the number is somewhat reduced.

THE DEANERY

The Choir School building is the gift of Mrs. J. Jarrett Blodgett in memory of her father, Mr. John Hinman Sherwood. The late Commodore Frederick G. Bourne, himself an old choir boy of Trinity Church and the Church of the Incarnation, has provided largely for the endowment of the school. A tablet in the porch reads:

**"In Faithful Memory of John Hinman Sherwood. Just, Upright, True. Erected by his daughter, 1912."**

## St. Faith's House

St. Faith's House (D. on plan) is the home of the New York Training School for Deaconesses, an independent corporation which was founded in 1890 by the late Rev. William Reed Huntington, D.D., and which occupies a site in the Cathedral Close by permission of the Trustees of the Cathedral. The building of Indiana limestone and brick is in Tudor Gothic architecture. It is the gift of Archdeacon Charles C. Tiffany in memory of his wife. The architects were Messrs. Heins & LaFarge.

## The Synod House

The Synod House (E. on plan), standing in the southwestern angle of the Close on the corner of Cathedral parkway and Amsterdam avenue, is the meeting place of the Diocesan Convention and other secular gatherings of the Diocese. It also contains the Bishop's office and the offices of the Suffragan Bishops. It is of Kingwood, W. Va., sandstone with pink tinges, quite unlike any other stone in the Cathedral group. The *Architecture* is pure French Gothic of the 13th century, Messrs. Cram & Ferguson being the Architects.

The *Western Entrance* is a very fine example of a mediaeval recessed porch in its architecture and an inter-

THE CHOIR SCHOOL

esting illustration of the progress of Civilization and Christianity in its sculptures. It contains 43 figures in the round and a relief of 12 figures in the tympanum. The key-note to the composition is the relief in the *Tympanum* representing Christ sending out his Disciples to baptize and teach all the nations of the world. Beneath this is the inscription:

"All power is given unto me in heaven and earth. Go ye therefore, and teach all nations, baptizing them in the name of the Father, and of the Son, and of the Holy Ghost; teaching them to observe all things whatsoever I have commanded you; and lo, I am with you alway, even unto the end of the world" (Mat. xxviii. 18-20).

The archivolt outside of the tympanum is composed of three ranges of Gothic niches in the voussoirs, containing 36 little figures in the round. The outer range represents 14 ancient and modern *Apostles of Christianity* as follows, beginning at the lowest figure on the left-hand side and reading upward to the center, and thence downward to the lowest right-hand figure: (1) Count Zinzendorf, 1700-1760, German reformer, founder of Moravian Brethren, missionary to American Indians; (2) St. Boniface, 680-755, Apostle of Germany; (3) St. Francis Xavier, 1506-1552, Apostle of the Indies, one of the founders of the Society of Jesus; (4) St. Denis, 3d century, Apostle of the Gauls, Patron Saint of France; (5) St. Olaf, 995-1030, Patron Saint and King of Norway; (6) St. Augustine, died 604, missionary to Britain, first Archbishop of Canterbury; (7) Innocent of Moscow, 1797-1879, Apostle of Alaska and Kamchatka, Archbishop of Moscow; (8) St. Patrick, circ. 372-460, Apostle and Patron Saint of Ireland; (9) John Eliot, 1604-1690, Apostle of American Indians, translator of Bible into Indian language; (10) St. Willibrod, 658-739, Apostle of the Frisians, Archbishop of Utrecht; (11) St. Cyril, 827-869, Apostle of the Slavs, inventor of the Cyrillic alphabet; (12) David Livingstone, 1813-1873,

THE SYNOD HOUSE

British explorer and missionary in Africa; (13) St. Columba, 521-597, Apostle of Caledonia; (14) Charles George Gordon, "Gordon Pasha," 1833-1885, British General, promoter of Christianity in China and Egypt. The 12 figures in the middle range represent the *Arts and Sciences.* In the same order they are: (1) Natural Science, man with microscope; (2) Sculpture, man with mallet and chisel; (3) Medicine, man with book and skull; (4) Literature, woman reading a book; (5) Chemistry, woman holding aloft a retort; (6) Industrial Art, man with vase; (7) Painting, man with palette; (8) Astronomy, man with globe; (9) Mathematics, man wearing spectacles and gown, holding cone and truncated pyramid; (10) Physics, woman with telephone; (11) Music, man with violoncello; (12) Architecture, man* holding model of building. The 10 figures in the innermost range represent the *Crafts and Industries,* as follows: (1) Bookbinding, man making a book; (2) Agriculture, man sowing seed; (3) Metal Industry, man pouring molten metal from ladle; (4) Textile Industry, woman with distaff and shuttle; (5) Navigation, sailor holding telescope with rope at feet; (6) Building, man laying brick; (7) Engineering, man holding tape measure; (8) Fishing, sailor with seine; (9) Mining, man with pickaxe and miner's cap; (10) Shoemaking, cobbler at his last. Below these, in niches in the splays and central pilaster of the door-way, are 7 larger figures representing *Seven Famous Christian Rulers* who have carried out the injunction in the tympanum, as follows, (left to right): (1) Emperor Constantine, once ruler of the Roman World and founder of Constantinople, who proclaimed religious toleration and presided over the council which adopted the Nicene Creed; (2) Charlemagne, King of the Franks, Emperor of the revived western Roman empire, who introduced Christianity into con-

---

* Ralph Adams Cram.

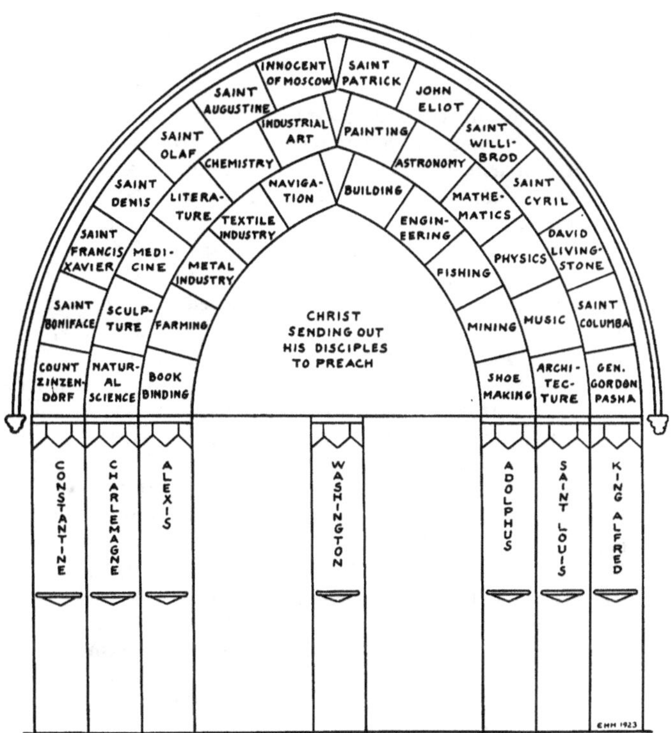


KEY TO FIGURES IN SYNOD HOUSE DOORWAY

*Outer Range:* Apostles of Christianity.
*Middle Range:* Arts and Sciences.
*Inner Range:* Crafts and Industries.
*Lower Range:* Famous Christian Rulers.

quered countries, maintained popular assemblies, and promoted science, art and letters; (3) Alexis, one of the ablest Emperors of Byzantium and friend of the Crusaders; (4, in center) George Washington, to whose character as Christian soldier, statesman and first President of the United States, attaches local interest from the fact that he commanded the American troops in the Battle of Harlem Heights which was fought partly on the ground occupied by the Cathedral Close; (5) Gustavus Adolphus, King of Sweden, one of the greatest generals, who, with his army in Germany, saved the cause of Protestantism in the Thirty Years War; (6) St. Louis, King of France, the most distinguished monarch of his age, who was noted for his piety, justice and mercy, and who died on a Crusade; and (7) Alfred the Great, King of Wessex, who bore the brunt of the Danish invasions and was a promoter of education and Christianity. The sculptures are by John Evans & Co. of Boston. The *Interior* decoration of the high roof and open timbers of the truss-work in polychrome is typical of the Middle Ages and the wood panelling is a reminder of 15th century work. The latter is by Messrs. Wm. F. Ross & Co., of Cambridge, Mass. The grisaille windows are by Mr. Charles J. Connick of Boston. The main hall, which seats 800 on the floor and 400 in the gallery, has a large pipe organ built by the Ernest M. Skinner Co. of Boston. The Undercroft (basement) is equipped for use as a refectory. In the main vestibule, over the outer doorway, is this inscription:

"To the Glory of God and for the Service of His People, This Synod House was Given in the year A. D. 1912, by John Pierpont Morgan and William Bayard Cutting."

## Open Air Pulpit

The Open Air Pulpit (F. on plan) standing in the midst of the Cathedral Close, is in the form of an open-work Gothic spire 40 feet high, built of Daytona stone, On its four sides are the usual symbols of the four Evangelists. The pulpit was designed by Messrs. Howells and Stokes and was presented by Miss Olivia Phelps Stokes.

## Organizations

The following organizations of men and women aid in the Cathedral work:

*The Diocesan Auxiliary to the Cathedral:* President, Mrs. Henry W. Munroe; Vice-Presidents, Mrs. Haley Fiske, Mrs. John Greenough, Mrs. W. M. V. Hoffman; Secretary, Mrs. Samuel Sloan; Assistant Secretary, Mrs. Courtlandt Nicoll; Treasurer, Mrs. Harold F. Hadden; Assistant Treasurer, the Farmers Loan & Trust Co.

*The Cathedral League:* President, Mr. John S. Rogers; Vice-President, Hon. Thomas C. T. Crain; Treasurer, Mr. Harry Pelham Robbins; Secretary, Dr. John B. Walker.

*The Laymen's Club:* President, Mr. Henry M. Sperry; Vice Presidents, Dr. George Stevenson, Col. Francis R. Appleton, Jr., and Mr. Herbert W. Smith; Treasurer, Mr. Charles P. Dietz; Secretary, Mr. J. Hardwick Stagg. The Laymen's Club was organized in 1908 and was incorporated in 1920, "to promote and stimulate interest in the influence, growth and completion of the Cathedral; to bring the Cathedral and its work more completely within the knowledge of the community; and to promote the general welfare of the Cathedral." Among its activities are the publication of this Guide Book and the Cathedral post-cards, the improvement of the Cathedral grounds, the assisting of a choir boy to complete in some well-known preparatory school his preparation for college, the training of the Cathedral Troop of Boy Scouts, the giving of free lectures, the ushering in the Cathedral, including the escorting of visitors in pilgrimages around the Cathedral, etc. The Club has also undertaken to raise the $100,000 needed for the marble pavement of the Nave.

*The Cathedral Ushers* are members of the Laymen's Club as stipulated in a resolution of the Cathedral Trustees passed April 25, 1911. The badge of the Ushers is a vesica-shaped gold medallion, having in the center an episcopal mitre, surrounded by the legend "Ecclesia Cathedralis S. Johannis Theologi;" suspended by a purple ribbon from a gold bar bearing the word "Usher."

## Publications

The following publications by the Laymen's Club may be procured at the Cathedral from the Verger or the Ushers, or will be sent by mail upon receipt of request, accompanied by remittance, sent to the Laymen's Club: *A Guide to the Cathedral Church of St. John the Divine in the City of New York,* (this book); price, in illuminated paper covers, 50 cents (by mail 60 cents); in purple cloth covers stamped with gold, $1.00 (by mail, $1.10). *The Cathedral: A Poem on the Building of the Cathedral Church of St. John the Divine,* by the author of the Guide Book; the story of the Cathedral in rhymed English heroic verse, with explanatory notes; 24 pages and cover; price, 25 cents. *Cathedral Post-Cards,* 20 different views, in sepia half-tone, in two sets of ten cards each; price 25 cents for each set of ten cards. *Photographs and Photogravures,* several views; price 25 and 50 cents each.

www.ingramcontent.com/pod-product-compliance
Lightning Source LLC
LaVergne TN
LVHW010611110826
845149LV00003B/870

* 9 7 8 1 4 1 8 1 8 7 1 5 6 *